How

Can

We

Make

This

Happen?

How Can We Make This Happen?

Successful Change
Through
Incentives and Trust

Nic Vine

Trenchant Books

Trenchant Books
8 Trenchard Street
London SE10 9PA
www.trenchantbooks.com

Published by Trenchant Books 2016

A CIP catalogue record for this book is
available from the British Library

Paperback   ISBN 978-0-9954766-0-8
eBook Mobi ISBN 978-0-9954766-1-5
eBook ePub ISBN 978-0-9954766-2-2

Printed by Amazon CreateSpace
eBook formatted by Bluewave Publishing

For Lesley and Mary

Contents

Notes for the Reader

You don't need to have *project*, *programme* or *change* in your job title to benefit from this book. Everybody is involved to some extent when change occurs; sometimes we lead change, sometimes we facilitate it, sometimes we participate, and sometimes change lands upon us.

This book captures what I have observed, experienced, learned, discovered and invented over the years, when running change projects and programmes myself, and when mentoring and coaching people in this science-cum-art. It is not a 'do this' instruction manual. My style is more along the lines of story-telling and discussion, to stimulate and enlighten your own thinking. Please take and use whatever works for you.

Men and women can be equally good, and sometimes bad, at being involved in change, so please read no significance into my usage of 'he' or 'she' in the text.

Each of Chapters 2 to 8 starts with a fictional story to illustrate the thrust of that chapter, using different formats of presentation; my hope is that they entertain you and draw you in. **Whilst naturally this whole book reflects my real-life experiences, the stories at the beginning of each chapter are fictional and any resemblance to real people or organisations is coincidental.**

For an explanation of my use of certain terms, please look at the Terminology section at the end of the book.

Acknowledgements

First and foremost I thank my wife, Lesley Curwen; she tirelessly encourages me, and spots plenty of errors whilst giving hugely constructive input on the shape and style of the narrative. All remaining errors are, of course, mine alone.

I could not write this without the large variety of working experiences, and so I owe thanks to very many colleagues in many organisations where I have worked over the last 20 years as an interim project, programme and change manager.

I also thank Jon Sibson and his colleagues in the Business Faculty at the University of Greenwich for letting me test-drive some of my content in my guest lectures and workshops with the undergraduates and postgraduates there.

Finally I thank Judith Harvey at RHE Media for her patient advice, and for guiding me over the finishing line to publication.

All trademarks are the property of their respective owners.

Prologue

Change management in some form has been going on since early humans first began to control their lives and their surroundings, perhaps some 500,000 years ago with the taming of fire, according to *History* edited by Adam Hart-Davis. The proactive management of change may go back some 5,000 years to the maturing of early societies and the Bronze Age that gave us effective tools and weapons. The intellectual management of change might be said to go back 500 years, to the beginning of the Renaissance. Change management as a discipline goes back less than 50 years, with a structured approach emerging around 1990. The first industry body was set up in 2004, and an internationally recognised qualification followed a few years later.

As with our technology advances, that is quite an acceleration. What we need to understand is that our social advances have been far less extreme, patchy even, so our incentives are largely still rooted in our relatively primitive past, and do not match up to our technical and organisational abilities. You might say that our tools have become better and exponentially better, whilst we have only become a little bit socially smarter.

So is everything really new and differently challenging in the 21st century, or does it just feel like that to each generation? What is different compared to the 20th, 19th, even 18th centuries? There was a huge change when the industrial revolution arrived, which occurred over about 50 years from 1780. Economic historians agree that it was the most important event in the history of humanity since the domestication of animals and plants. It certainly had a world-wide impact.

When our current age is viewed as history, then the digital revolution, or possibly the information or communication revolution, will be seen as an equally important 'event'. Interestingly, it too has been running for around 50 years since the early 1960s and one could argue that digital technology has matured now. No doubt it will continue to evolve, just as the machines did in the 19th century. So is there some consistency here, in that a significant world-wide advance in human ingenuity and capability took two generations to mature? Of course it is notoriously difficult to call the end of a revolution when you are living in it, and so we must leave confirmation of that to the historians of the future.

It may be that the pace of change experienced in the context of an individual 'common man' in these two revolutions is similar. The difference in the digital revolution, and particularly now in the 21st century, is the mass communication it enables; this means we have a hugely increased *awareness* of the changes – we are constantly bombarded by a blizzard of information, advice, opinion and instruction on what we should, and should not, think and do. This global awareness also acts as an amplifier for more and faster innovation, and so maybe this time the revolution will just keep on rolling.

Yet in all this, the human animal is instinctively, emotionally and motivationally the same animal he or she was in previous centuries, perhaps all the way back beyond the Romans, the Greeks, even the Ancient Egyptians. That is what we have to understand and manage, in order to achieve successful and sustainable changes within any organisation. It is the elephant in the room – so huge and obvious that either we do not see it, or we prefer to ignore it in the hope that it will go away. We do so at our peril.

1 Big Picture

*"**If we do not take change by the hand,
it will surely take us by the throat**."*
Winston Churchill

Winston Churchill captured beautifully the challenge we all face in our personal lives, in the organisations where we study and work, and in society at large. Let us not be uncomprehending victims, taken by the throat. Instead let us understand, embrace and manage change, to benefit ourselves and those around us.

My fundamental premise is that people are the most difficult part of change, and that for any change to succeed we have to give each person involved an individual reason for positive action or acceptance. These reasons come from people's individual incentives, and the network of trust between people. Understanding, influencing & aligning incentives and establishing, building & maintaining trust are the cornerstones of achieving successful change.

Your incentive

You're still here – good – and so I assume you are open to some ideas and insights on how to make successful, sustainable changes with minimum stress.

Let's imagine a scenario; you haven't bought this book yet, you are in a shop, browsing, and decided to check out the style in the first chapter. Good plan. So, to discover a win-win situation for you, please keep reading … while you walk slowly and carefully over to the queue for the checkout … avoiding collisions with fellow shoppers and vertiginous display stands. If the checkout queue is long then not only do you have something to read while you wait, you also have some more time to decide whether you want to buy me or not – after all, you can always step out of the queue - and you have saved time by making your assessment in the queue rather than over by the bookshelf. If however the queue is short, you are probably at the till already … so pay the nice person, and feel good about having made an interesting purchase without wasting time queuing.

So what did I do there? I provided incentives for action, with an opt-out along the way, and without asking for your trust because I have not earned it yet. Incentives and trust come up again and again throughout this book – and there are many incentives other than money.

Your broader incentives in picking this book, I imagine, are to explore it for ideas and advice that will be useful to you. Let me just say at the start that often this business of participating in change is not easy, and it *is* ok to under-deliver sometimes. We can learn a lot from when things go wrong, and it is better to fail occasionally than not to try at all.

A swift tour of the book

My scope here is the broadest possible, including any kind of change affecting any type of organisation (see the Terminology section for definitions), whether the change be in branding, product, business process, technology, governance structure, financing, physical building or a hundred other aspects of how and why a group of people work together.

After this chapter that sets out the Big Picture, we look at the '**Me**' aspects and discuss the understanding and managing of incentives and trust. This is what people respond to, and there are different people types with different responses. 'Hearts and minds' may be a familiar phrase, and it is the key to effective working, yet achieving a strong sense of belonging across a team of essentially selfish animals can be quite a challenge.

Then to form a structure and a plan that will deliver as expected, we need to **start at the end**. It is essential to define measurable benefits, to allow for a range of acceptable outcomes, and to have a shared understanding of where we are going and why. This often requires us to speak truth to power, in order to have an achievable combination of function, quality, timescale and cost.

Implementing this structure calls for the use of **strategies and tactics** and a clear idea of the difference between them. High quality two-way communication is essential in building up trust across all the participants. Trust is a huge amplifier for action; with trust established we can move management mountains.

There are many different types and sizes of changes, of course, and correspondingly many **different dynamics** or ways of going about the implementation. It is healthy to examine the consequences of doing nothing, or at least waiting a while. On the other hand an elephantine change is often better done in the optimal sequence of bites, to avoid it overwhelming us.

Another vital piece of context in which to work is the **pressure from both the past and the future**, outside the timescale of this change. Expectations that have been inherited are dangerous. Lessons from previous changes must be examined for relevance. Sustainability of the change's benefits must be part of the success measures.

Even the best-planned change will suffer **blockers and distractions**; it is the human nature challenge again.

We must always be on the alert for disruption, intentional or otherwise. Problems can be managed, risks mitigated, external factors contained; it is uncertainty that saps morale and breeds indecision.

In the end we will succeed if we **make people happy**.

The nature of change

We all know what we mean by Change, don't we? Ok, let's make sure – here is my broad definition: "transitioning individuals, teams, and organisations from a current state to a required future state, by altering, adding or removing some components in the existing status quo".

Now, what do we mean by Successful Change? The obvious answer is that the change delivers the expected results or outcomes. This means that first there must be some well-defined expectations, and that they must be achievable, and second that there must be a practical way of measuring them. Furthermore 'successful' needs to include 'relevant' and 'sustainable', so that the benefit of the change is both real at the time of delivery and maintained over time. All too often a team proudly delivers the specified change, only to find that while they have been sweating away the world has moved on and it's no longer relevant, or that within days or weeks the benefit of the change begins to degrade, to slip and slide away. To guard against this requires strategy, communication, scenario planning and clear-sighted governance.

So why Incentives and Trust? Because, I'll say it again, the understanding and usage of these concepts are to me the cornerstones of building successful change. In my view it is all about the people and what drives them, what makes them want to participate and support ... or to sabotage and block.

The challenge across all industries and scenarios is that, to be successful, any change must be embraced by all the relevant people, everyone who is affected in some way (often referred to as stakeholders) – that means understanding, supporting and sustaining. All organisations wrestle with this at some level.

There is no single 'magic bullet' answer to getting any change 'right'. What is highly desirable, and practical, is to have a common, consistent & visible framework for action which is adapted to individual circumstances

It is a common perception that people in general dislike change, and that they prefer things to stay as they are. Yet it is not Change as such that people dislike, it is Uncertainty or Bad News or Disruption, and these are relative or contextual to each individual. Conversely there are people who are happy to use change as a smoke-screen or excuse for poor performance. In addition there are people who revel in change, who excel in managing the journey from Here to There, and who get bored with regular, normal operation. These latter are our local champions, our embedded entrepreneurs.

The use of layers of information, and the same messages presented in different ways, can reduce the apparent complexity. This improves a sense of belonging, and of playing a positive part in a beneficial change. Finding the positives does us all a power of good.

Structuring change

"The one constant is change" is a facile and frankly misleading observation. My apologies to the descendants of François de la Rochefoucauld, but there it is.

Equally trite to my mind is "Nothing endures but change", attributed to Heraclitus of Ephesus, a Greek philosopher known for his doctrine of change being central to the universe.

I think the talk of continuous or all-pervasive change and the increasing rate of change is not helpful in organisations. These statements have been used for many decades, and were no doubt used in the industrial revolution. Today they are often used either to hide poor performance or to promote services and products that apparently assist in making change. Caveat emptor.

The particular danger of 'continuous change' is that it debilitates an organisation, demoralises individuals and sucks resources & budget. At worst, it is a Ponzi scheme that funds the next change with the savings from the current one, never delivering a penny to the bottom line.

Whilst change may look continuous when viewed from a distance, the up close view must see a sequence of discrete changes that each follow a simple 5-part cycle:

beginning - middle - end - review - sustain

Later we will discuss a variety of types of change, including 'incremental' which is the acceptable face of continual change, and not our main focus. Let's stick with the view that after a change we want a period of stability during which we reap the benefits.

It is worth making the point here that by 'change' we do not just mean altering something that currently exists. It could be doing something entirely new, because that still has an impact on the status quo, affects the people in the organisation, and alters the organisation's connection to the world around it. Alternatively it could be less than altering; it could be simply repairing or replacing so that afterwards everything is the same – there is still disruption, there are still costs and risks, it is still a change that needs managing.

Finally, beware of the 'change is good' mantra. It is not universally true. Stopping the wrong Changes can be as important as starting the right Changes.

Drivers for change

Very broadly the drivers of change that we see in the world about us are in four areas; physical, social, technological and commercial ... the biggest of which is commercial. The only one of these four areas not overwhelmingly influenced by humanity itself is the physical. Even there you would have to say that climate change (in the strong balance of scientific opinion) and energy needs are the primary instigators of physical change, caused by humanity. So what is left? Solar flares, volcanic eruptions, earthquakes (and resultant tsunamis) and the very occasional sizeable meteor. Apart from those, we are doing it all to ourselves.

This may be blindingly obvious, perhaps so much so that we don't see it. I believe that most individual humans feel that most change is thrust upon them, yet collectively we are the cause of almost all of it. This is worth thinking about, in terms of how we view the world. I contend that the feeling of having change thrust upon us, as an individual or group, is the single biggest blocker to achieving successful change.

In 2015 a third annual *Survey On Change* across organisations large and small was reported in the Impact Journal Issue 31. It was run by Impact Executives, a provider of interim managers to organisations around the world, and the survey was completed by over 250 business leaders across more than 15 countries. 86% said their company was experiencing more change than ever before; this is a very similar percentage to the previous surveys, although it is not clear whether it was exactly the same companies, nor what timescale they were using as a comparison. The natural business reporting cycle is a year, and so one could infer that in 2015 they experienced more change than 2014 which was more change than ever before. Whilst it is a subjective assessment and a qualitative analysis, and so should be treated with some caution, there appears to be a steady escalation in perceived change.

Back to the question, then, in a slightly modified form: why are we visiting all this change on ourselves? The answer is, I believe, about as big as the question, and is a combination of population evolutions, technology advances, natural world understanding, and the increasing sophistication of societies and economies.

This affects the developed world as much as the developing world. This isn't just business, or indeed organisations in general. It is addressing human nature and therefore is relevant to personal changes, voluntary activities, sports & pastimes. It is human nature to strive for personal betterment.

In the narrower context of organisations, ask the same question; and the answer is a filtered version of those world-wide drivers, which translates into more social and commercial opportunities, more sophisticated competition, and more complex business models.

So with our clever thinking and fantastic tools we are roaring along with hardly a backward glance. There is a lot of loose talk about 'learning lessons' from previous changes and yet we are, in my experience, very poor at doing so. The pressure is always to move forward.

The biggest picture of all, in the human context, is our whole planet. This includes our vast population of satellites as far as 22,300 miles above the surface. (I think it's fair to say that despite the litter of equipment on the Moon and on Mars, humanity is a long way from messing up the environment outside our own planet.) With the insistent references to globalisation throughout the economy and the environment, it sometimes feels as though all changes need to be viewed in this context. Perhaps it is not a bad default starting point. In other words, don't think "what do we need to include" but rather "what can we justifiably exclude" when thinking through the scope, risks and consequences.

Your expectations

This book is about the philosophy, psychology, strategies and techniques of making successful changes. It is about recognising and understanding the people factors that affect change, and using that understanding to succeed, participate or simply observe with less stress than is often incurred.

This is not a conventional 'how to' book with detailed instructions, nor is it an evangelical tract exhorting you to follow the one true method. Think of it as somewhere between a workshop and a fireside chat. You have a much higher likelihood of success if the knowledge, skills and experience conveyed by this book are applied by you, intelligently and selectively, to your specific situations, rather than if you faithfully follow a flowchart of rigid methodology.

I am making assertions, and discussing why and how I reached them ... and in the process I will either secure your wholehearted or grudging agreement, or you will end up disagreeing with me. Either way it should be stimulating, and in any case I would be pleased for you to contact me and tell me why you agree or disagree.

You can if you wish pick any philosophy or belief system and find some business books to support it – people are very good at rationalising and advancing any particular position. Those books often assume you've got the authority, responsibility and bandwidth to make the change. But what if you are an over-loaded middle manager with a distracted boss and dysfunctional teams? What if you are a subject matter expert who has just been given responsibility for managing a project? What if you are a team member who feels disoriented by what is happening around you? Then you need some insights into why and how things happen ... or don't happen.

So what is different about this book? I'm saying this is my experience, these are my views and suggestions, and you may find them helpful. I cannot provide specific answers to all the situations that you have faced, are facing or will face. What I can do is identify the questions you could ask, and the tests you should apply to the answers, and in some cases the generic nature of those answers.

You will find me talking about 'fit-for-purpose' quite often. This is an essential yet simple concept, that guards against over-engineering and mismatched expectations. When something is fit-for-purpose it is sufficient for the task without skimping and without over-doing it. If you need to tighten a nut on your bicycle, a simple spanner is fit-for-purpose where pliers would be risky and a torque wrench would be unnecessary expense.

One more thing. I am wary of using numerical analysis to validate arguments. A proper understanding of what is 'cause' and what is 'effect' is essential to good management, and numbers can very easily distort this. The book called *The Tiger That Isn't* by Michael Blastland & Andrew Dilnot does a splendid job of explaining how numbers are used, misused and abused in every walk of modern day life.

Takeaways

- successful change delivers clear outcomes, with measurable and sustainable benefits
- the understanding and usage of incentives and trust are the cornerstones of change
- there is no single 'magic bullet' answer to getting any change 'right'
- it is not Change as such that people dislike, it is Uncertainty or Bad News or Disruption
- stopping the wrong Changes can be as important as starting the right Changes
- think of this book as somewhere between a workshop and a fireside chat
- these are my experiences, views and suggestions, and you may find them helpful

2 What is in it for Me?

Tom held his head in his hands, shoulders slumped, in a momentary loss of self-control. It had been a tough week – well, they all were, but perhaps this one was tougher than most. Now it was time to take the decision to end it all.

"We didn't get the deal" Chas had said yesterday, reporting back on his meeting with the top honcho in the one company that looked like a real possibility for partnership. "It's not the same people that I knew back in the day" he'd continued "they all seem like teenagers."

Tom thought back to just 18 months ago. It had all started in such entrepreneurial style, with a chance conversation at a party; that serendipitous moment when three very different people discovered they had a common goal, and needed each other to make it happen. At least it had seemed that simple at the time. Chas, an established musician, had an online business idea but little interest in running a business. Tom, a freelance business manager, was looking for a start-up idea and knew very little about the music industry. Elena, a software company director, had some programmers sitting idle due to a delayed project. Between them they could build a terrific business.

The buzz of the phone jolted Tom out of his reverie. It was Michael from the business advisory company, who had been chasing him for days. "Hi, hope it's all going well, I just wanted to square away that last invoice of ours, just so we can finalise the grant from the Enterprise Board, you know, just keep it all sweet" Michael chatted away. He meant that if Tom didn't pay then Michael wouldn't get the matching money from the council. Looking back Tom realised that Michael's company had provided perfectly credible and sensible marketing and financial planning work – however they weren't into shared responsibility for Chas and Tom's business. Michael's company needed cashflow which meant timely invoices and the brownie points with the local authority that would help it grow.

No sooner had Tom made some positive noises to satisfy Michael than the phone buzzed again. It was Chas drawling "so what d'you think, man, let's run another couple months – we can kick up some new website interest through the live gigs I set up, they're great fun". Yeah, man, thought Tom sourly, you have your fun with the musicians while I wrestle with the lack of money coming in.

Tom's next call was to Elena, who for a minor shareholding in this notional business had uncomplainingly developed some pretty neat software. "Hi Elena, how's it going ... yeah, good, but listen I'm cancelling any further requests for software modifications, we need to put the whole thing on ice for a while, you know we talked about this a while back" the guilt was making Tom gabble. "Ok, understood" said Elena in her usual measured way "my guys are getting busy again now anyway. I just need your letter giving permission for us to use the software in other projects. You know you had us develop a lot of very useful stuff – I hadn't realised the music business was that complicated." No, thought Tom, and it isn't really, it was me getting carried away with creating a beautiful interactive web service before we'd proved anyone would pay for it. Because I had the freedom to design a system just how I wanted it.

In a final moment of reflection Tom realised that none of them had felt a belonging with the whole business. Instead they'd each worked hard in their respective comfortable corners and just assumed it would all come together. Damn!

After the big picture discussions in the first chapter, we now get to the heart of the matter. My fundamental assertion is that the human being is a selfish animal, and all incentives and actions should be seen in the perspective of self-interest in the broadest sense.

Of course self-interest is not often overt, or even conscious, and of course there are exceptions ... although I suspect they are rarer than we might think or wish. In the fiction above, no-one is trying to disadvantage someone else and they know they need to work together, and yet each is driven by their own interests.

It is not the tools, materials, technology or methodology that is the most important factor in one or more people achieving anything ... it is the psychology. People are incentivised by self-interest that comes in many layers and guises. David McWilliams, the Irish economist, said when launching Kilkenomics 2013 "economics is not about maths, it's about people – people like you and me, and what we do".

We are at heart, or rather in the head, a primitive lot still rooted in our survival instincts, and this causes difficulties in organisations, societies and civilisations. Yet education, communication and belonging to a community do help us to transcend the primitive, if not the self entirely.

We are not lacking in ideals and aspirations for good health, equality, fairness, peace and a supportive society. Yet everywhere you look our actions and achievements let us down – we do not live up to our own expectations and aspirations.

Now that may have raised the 'why not' question in your mind, and it is a good question. I have to tell you that I don't know, and I don't believe there is 'one answer', although there is material in here that may help the thinking. My point is simply that it underpins all that we do, and I'm discussing it here to lay the ground for all that follows.

So this chapter looks at the challenges posed by Human Nature, examines Incentives and how they work, explores People Types, considers the dynamics and dangers of Trust, and finally discusses how to reach both Hearts & Minds.

Human nature

We seem to have over-evolved, in that we do not appear to use all the apparent capability of our brains. How that squares with the accepted Darwinian principles of evolution is an interesting question to which I have no answer (or it is certainly a different book). It is clear to me that technological progress, and our ability to modify our environment, has run far ahead of our emotional and societal progress. We fight more sophisticated wars, though interestingly with far fewer visible rules than of old.

illustration: wired planet and dirty water

Satellites, the internet and mobile phone networks have wired the planet ... and yet 9% of the population do not have access to safe water, and over 30% do not have access to adequate sanitation (Wateraid, 2016). How can it be, that we put aerial photographs, tweeting and chatting ahead of drinking water and sanitary improvements – would we do that in our own backyard? I think not. But there's the clue – 'backyard' – for we are territorial animals, and our instinct is for preservation of self, family, community, society, country in that order. This is relevant because there are backyards in organisations too – often they are littered with them. A backyard is under 'my' control, a village square is under 'our' control, but beyond that we delegate control (in a democracy) or relinquish control (in an autocracy).

baggage

As discussed in the Prologue, there is a sharply accelerating history in the scope and consequence of the changes we are wreaking on ourselves, our organisations, our societies and more recently our planet.

Michael Sherman in *The Mind of the Market* contrasts our hunter-gatherer past (from 100,000 to 10,000 years ago) with what he calls the consumer-trader model today. There may have been a few more models in between. Hunter-gatherers took what was available to them, as the name says, albeit in increasingly sophisticated ways. Then came the first steps in managing their food, becoming an agricultural society through the farming of plants and animals. This was mainly at a subsistence/self-sufficiency level until the Industrial Revolution, when there was a huge shift to cash crops for trade on a world-wide basis. Consumer-trader could simply describe those exchanging different surplus foodstuffs. In the 21st century we consume things like electricity and trade things like ideas, while there are hundreds of millions who are still in survival mode. In evolutionary terms it is but a moment since we were all hunter-gatherers in survival mode, and on a bad day that shows through even in the most sophisticated societies.

Some years ago I began to outline a hierarchy in the fundamentals for quality of life, starting with the preservation of life (air, water, food, shelter) and moving up to enjoying life (physical ease, partner, social belonging, intellectual stimulus) and then up to controlling life (money and power). Then I discovered it had already been done, as with so many bright ideas; Abraham Maslow proposed the 'hierarchy of needs' in his 1943 paper *A Theory of Human Motivation*. (Note that I use 'incentive' throughout rather than 'motivation'. They mean the same thing.)

Maslow Hierarchy

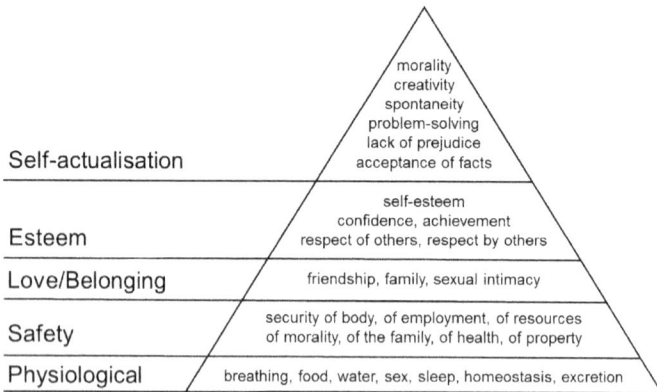

http://commons.wikimedia.org/wiki/File:Maslow's_hierarchy_of_needs.png

Although through the decades there have been a variety of criticisms and variations, Maslow's hierarchy remains a popular framework for thinking about incentives, especially in management training. A BBC

World Service 'Health Check' programme in August 2013 identified the equivalent layers of needs within an organisation.

Step 5 - Self-actualisation	Opportunities for creativity and personal growth, promotion
Step 4 - Esteem	Fancy job title, recognition of achievements
Step 3 - Social	Good team atmosphere, friendly supervision
Step 2 - Safety	Safe working conditions, job security
Step 1 - Physiological	Salary, decent working environment

Once the basic needs are established, incentives in organisations are often relative rather than absolute, in terms of competition from within and outside the organisation. It is worth thinking about the organisation's incentives as well as that of the individuals – when they are badly misaligned there is a high probability of trouble.

One of the criticisms of Maslow is that he stated an individual cannot focus on a higher step until the lower steps are established, and clearly that is too rigid; there are plentiful examples of impoverished artists producing wonderful work, of downtrodden activists achieving social change, and of people helping others (step 5) whilst not having their own steps 3 and 4 fully in place. That said, it is a useful reminder that someone with a seriously ill partner may find it difficult to be an effective team member, and someone whose house is flooded may have trouble hitting their targets at work.

Can it really be the case that in the 21st century we are still behaving like animals driven by the distinction between predator and prey, between hunting and being hunted? The Economist used this metaphor in commenting on the actions of Santander Bank in 2008 when within a couple of weeks it switched from rapacious predator on financial institutions staggering and wounded by the financial crisis, to defensive increases in capital to avoid being marginalised by other large European banks. Another way to illustrate this is the story of two tourists who find themselves facing a leopard; as one quickly puts on running shoes the other says "that's no good, you can't run faster than a leopard" to which the first replies "I know, but I only need to run faster than you".

How is this huge and sticky subject of the human condition relevant, you may ask? It is relevant because everything we do is governed by human nature, and frankly civilisation is a very thin skin. Scratch that skin and you quickly see primal instincts and urges which have little to do with our complex 21st century societies, and much more to do with 'self' from survival upwards.

selfishness

Humans have developed emotional intelligence, without which our complex societies could not function. It is both a benefit and a burden.

I have contended that we as individuals do operate almost wholly on a self-interest basis. There is a wide range of self-interest, from being crowned as absolute monarch at one end, to a brief moment of pleasure or duty emotion at the other. Truly altruistic actions, where those taking action perceive no benefit or pleasure, are very rare. Even those actions with no tangible benefit usually have an intangible 'feel-good' benefit. The only truly self-less acts are where we suffer a net dis-benefit from our action, and I suggest this is rarer still.

Let's take a simple example of a queue at the supermarket check-out. You have a trolley full and behind you is a harassed dad with an unhappy toddler and just 6 items. So you let him go in front of you, thereby delaying your shopping by a minute. Is that an altruistic act? I suggest not, because you get the benefit of a "thanks" from the man, your feel-good from helping someone, and you only have the child's tantrums bouncing off your ears for one minute instead of the ten minutes to process your trolley. And all it cost you was a minute. Now reverse the example; you have 6 items and the dad and the tantrums behind you have the full trolley. Are you going to invite him to go in front? I doubt it, because the ratio of reward to pain is not great enough.

I admit that there are some examples of truly self-less acts, and the ones that spring to my mind are generally in extreme situations of conflict or physical danger. I may be contentious in saying that acts of heroism in the armed forces, throughout history, can be explained by the training and extremely tight bonding of small groups which reduces the individualism to a minimum. I will further stick my neck out by suggesting that members of armed forces do not join up thinking "I could die" but rather have the attitude "it happens but it won't happen to me". The person wading into a raging river in an attempt to rescue someone has not thought "if I die through saving them that's ok" – they are much more likely to think "there's a risk here but I can do this", or in the case of a parent they don't think rationally about it all, they just react instinctively.

There are those, such as Mary Midgley in her book *The Solitary Self: Darwin and the Selfish Gene* who argue that human society depends on cooperation, compromise and sociability, and that the incentives for this are beyond explicit self-interest.

My definition of self-interest is broader – I am including what you might call secondary self-interest where the benefit or just the feel-good outweighs the dis-benefit. Cooperation is necessary because in a complex society we cannot do everything for ourselves individually, and compromise and sociability arise out of this cooperation; none of that reduces the self-interest that is driving all actions. The point is to understand and allow for this fundamental factor in human society, in the same way that we need food and toilet breaks – it is how we are made.

Cooperation increases when there is a simple, common goal, and even more so with a common threat, the prime example in Britain being the World Wars. There is in the British psyche a memory of all pulling together, although in reality even the war periods had their racketeers who took advantage of the situation. Much more recently the Coalition Government elected in 2010 tried to convince the UK population that "we are all in it together" in managing and recovering from the latest economic crisis – presumably to encourage our cooperation.

Let's pull back from death, destruction and financial purgatory to the slightly safer ground of staff in an organisation. Can you think of an example where someone has sacrificed their interests for the sake of someone else or some other organisation? No? I cannot. Now can you think of examples where someone has promoted their own self-interest at the expense of someone else or some other organisation? Of course, a thousand times yes.

positive pessimism

It is hard to under-estimate the power of positive thinking, and yet we are all too ready to look on the negative side. Some might refer to our typical reaction to change as scepticism, or cynicism, or even paranoia.

Being positive is not the same as being optimistic. Anyone managing change needs an internal streak of pessimism in order to anticipate problems and properly manage expectations. In the story at the beginning of this chapter, Elena has at least planned for a negative outcome in that her investment is software that can be put to other uses.

Positive thinking and confidence can build a virtuous circle – even when there are no secure foundations. This can be a good thing for the entrepreneur who is convincing someone to invest in her ideas, and with that investment the foundations can then be built. It can also be a bad thing, such as in a Ponzi investment structure where there never are any foundations and once someone points out the unsustainability (fraud) the whole thing collapses very quickly.

There is another trap for the unwary, which is thinking when under pressure "it will be better next week/month/quarter". It always *looks* as though it will be better, because we have a less clear view of the details then, and we have the optimistic view that factors causing the current pressure will not recur. The fact is that in order to have less pressure in the future we have to do something now. Proactively manage expectations; if we are good at our job, no-one can ask more of us than a realistic commitment given the circumstances.

I find this old maxim very useful: expect the best and plan for the worst.

beliefs and desires

Managers and Boards all have a tendency to make 'statements of desire'. They state the outcome they want in a confident and positive manner, and assume it is do-able. They want a change to happen, by a specified date, yet they don't have the knowledge, skills or experience to gauge the achievability of that change at a detailed level. Ideally they engage with an open mind with those who do have the necessary knowledge, skills & experience, and adjust their statements of desire in the light of that expert feedback. Far more frequently they make the statement a few times and then just assume it is achievable, or worse still that it has already been done.

There is a reason for this. Often people rise to a senior position in an organisation because they are confident and decisive; they don't have much self-doubt. Now just because they have risen to a level where they cannot see or know all the detail, does not mean that self-doubt conveniently appears in their mind. So they make their statements that something should happen just so, and they believe them.

A new senior manager introduced himself to my programme team by saying that he had "strong beliefs, loosely held", meaning that he was pretty sure he knew what was needed, however he was prepared to listen and adjust according to others' viewpoints. This is a great combination of leadership and openness, and is sadly all too rare.

The common phrase "On Time and To Budget" is the clarion call for 'good project management'. It is all very well if:

1. you have done the work before, so have precisely relevant experience
2. you have complete control over all the factors
3. you have expertise in analysis and planning
4. you have doubled the numbers that your analysis first suggested

This last bullet point may seem like a joke. I assure you that it is not. We have an unfortunate predilection for under-estimating complex work where we are not very practised at it. It is not so much optimism as blind faith, or worse still simply matching against the management's statement of desire, telling them what they want to hear.

The majority of straightforward engineering projects, a new building or a new bridge, are delivered close to time and budget. We have been doing those projects for many hundreds of years, and through cumulative experience combined with formal tuition and professional bodies of knowledge we have got the hang of it.

Do something different though and the result is far less predictable.

The nature of technology engineering, for instance, is that we are pretty much always doing something different, because both the underlying technology and our inventive uses for it are evolving so rapidly. It is my honest belief that if people really knew in advance how much large software developments were going to cost, most of them would never be started. And yet of course they are useful when they finally get there – so perhaps our blindness or optimism does serve a purpose.

amplifiers

Technology is a very strong amplifier. Used well, it significantly improves the cost, time, function and quality of the outcome. Use it even a little bit badly, and it significantly degrades one or more of those factors, and can easily derail the whole project.

Trust is a softer type of amplifier. It is much harder to measure and assess than technology, yet it is equally powerful. Have you seen the change in attitude, morale and productivity when a trusted manager does something to betray that trust? The swing can be dramatic. Unquestioning support becomes rabid suspicion in a very short time.

Amplifiers are often in the supporting functions of an organisation, things that can either make life easy or hard for staff and which can spiral into attitudes about the whole organisation. Even something as simple as the ergonomics and cleanliness of a building can be an amplifier through affecting staff morale and the general sense of belonging and wellbeing.

If an organisation needs to do something for the common good and yet individuals rail against it, this has to be positively handled. Take the example of a 'clean desk' policy for security reasons. Perfectly sensible. Yet a number of brilliant people won't comply because they simply cannot organise themselves that way. If we penalise them somehow they will spread their unrest and become demoralised. Far better to assist them, not by making special exceptions which irritates other staff but by providing practical help

can we fix it?

No, we cannot fix human nature. So watch out. All of the above are happening all of the time.

It may seem from the **positive pessimism** and the **beliefs & desires** segments above that I am contradicting myself, by asserting that we are in that habit of negative thinking, and yet also we are far too optimistic. These ideas are not opposites and can be reconciled. Our tendency is to be pessimistic about the impact of changes upon us, and optimistic about our ability to generate change that will impact others. It is like looking through different ends of the same telescope.

In many walks of life we truly celebrate the spontaneity, inventiveness and courage of the human spirit. Yet when we try to make a change in an organisation it can get in the way, trip us, ruin our plans.

Incentives drive everything

The single common factor across all change in all organisations and societies is people; and people can be very difficult, unpredictable, time-consuming, expensive, even dangerous – yet what we cannot do is get rid of them all! People take, and avoid, action based upon a complex mix of incentives that differ from one group to another and one individual to another. What we must do is understand their incentives.

illustration: freaky economics

In the second book by Steven Levitt & Stephen Dubner, *Superfreakonomics*, incentives are really the substrate for all the action; it is fascinating how people's real incentives are misunderstood, and how unintended consequences arise. Levitt & Dubner show that the ineffectiveness of the 'war on drugs' is due to focusing on closing suppliers (dealers), which creates a scarcity that drives prices up, which in turn attracts new suppliers. Hard for government perhaps, yet a focus on penalties for users would decrease demand and gradually close the market. When searching for terrorists through profiling, they suggest looking for people who have dependents but no life insurance – they don't buy it because it won't pay out when they blow themselves up.

The book also explains how Professor John List disproved the altruism theory prevalent up to 2005 wherein people in lab experiments appeared to take actions that benefited others when given simple choices. List ran real-life experiments instead of laboratory-based ones, with more complex choices. The real world is harder to manage for meaningful experiments yet that is where stuff happens and the lab will always be different because it's a lab. He showed that when people had more information their apparent altruism faded away.

Incentives make the world go round – it is why individuals do things from getting up in the morning to creating a world-leading organisation.

As we have seen when examining the human condition, the primary, over-riding incentive is self-interest in all its many shades and guises. The major exceptions to that are in highly-trained fighting forces, and in family; both of those special dynamics are outside the scope of this book.

Within the wide-ranging scope of organisations covered here, self-interest is the key to understanding people's incentives for action or indeed lack of action. Understanding incentives allows us to communicate in optimal ways, to anticipate and plan for problems, to modify or even create incentives, to influence people's thinking and priorities, and thereby to participate in successful change.

Whilst that may sound deceptively simple, self-interest operates in many layers, many forms, and many timescales; winkling out an individual's self-interests in the context of a given change in a particular organisation is often quite difficult, especially as we cannot really walk up to them and ask the bald question. If we did, we would be unlikely to get an accurate or comprehensive answer – they may not even consciously know it themselves. On top of that we might find ourselves without a job soon afterwards.

assumptions bad, analysis good

It is a common and popular claim that people dislike change, even that this dislike is rooted in a loss of comfort with the familiar that dates back to our primitive roots. No doubt this is true to some extent. It is also worth considering, though, that change is not always a transition from comfort into discomfort.

Sometimes there is an uncomfortable or negative situation already, where change to resolve or at least improve the situation will be welcomed. At other times there may be a better situation to be reached which is hard to see or keep in mind whilst going through the pains of the changes required to get there.

It is dangerous to make sweeping general assumptions, and much better to think through where people are at in their minds and how have they got there. Then think to what extent do they already want to move on, or what route they would prefer, and how much help they need to understand both the route and the end goal in their own context.

illustration: time & money

Charlie Munger, a partner of legendary investor Warren Buffet, gave a lecture at the Harvard Business School in 1995 entitled *The Psychology of Human Misjudgement*. It became a celebrated and widely-referenced lecture wherein he lists 24 standard causes of human misjudgement, and the first cause is under-recognition or misunderstanding of incentives. Munger uses as his main example the classic Fedex night shift case. Fedex were paying the night shift workers by the hour, the shift was not finishing its work on time and the logistics were falling apart. After considering a lot of possible reasons, the management had the bright idea of changing the incentive through paying them by the shift and they were free to go home once the work was completed. Instead of spinning the work out to earn the maximum, the workers now sped up to minimise the time spent earning the fixed amount. Problem apparently solved.

To my mind, this example as cited by Munger and others is over-simplified. The first concern when moving to a time incentive is that the quality falls – in this case parcels could be misdirected, leaving someone else to sort out the mess. So it's not quite as straightforward as replacing one incentive with another; safeguards need to be added to ensure other problems are not created as a consequence.

conflicts

It is quite possible for the incentives for different individuals or groups to be at odds. They may all be positive, yet also be mutually exclusive. In this case compromise is called for.

It is also important to think about the opposite to incentives, namely constraints and disincentives.

Disincentives are the stick where incentives are the carrot. Most organisations employ some combination of the two, and if any thought has gone into it they should reinforce each other.

Constraints are a very common occurrence. They may be systematic, such as external regulations, or they may be local to the project, such as a restricted budget.

Whenever some combination of the above work against each other, the individual or team will be conflicted. Even if there is no elegant solution to such a conflict, which is often the case, the stress of the situation can be eased if the conflict is recognised and discussed.

In some cases it may be a question of suffering local pain for the greater good. Or short-term pain for long-term gain. Then it is a question of containment, of managing and mitigating the effect or impact of the pain. In my experience it is usually best to use maximum openness and transparency, to let everyone see and understand the pain and put it into context.

When transformation is required across a large organisation there is often the following conundrum with no perfect solution. The Executive Team should operate solely with the organisation's best interests as top priority; sadly, I have rarely seen this happen. Instead their top priority is advancing, or at least protecting, their own 'backyard' – their division, section or department – because that is how they are incentivised. So the only person with a panoptic (organisation-wide) incentive is the CEO. In which case the Transformation Director has to operate at the CEO level, which makes her a perceived threat to everyone, including the CEO. Conflicts galore. Yet the panoptic remit is essential for the transformation director. The challenge remains that she will have responsibility beyond their authority, and thus will have to create effective, ego-less partnerships with the Executive Team. The organisation can help in this by ensuring that the Executive Team members are both tactically and strategically incentivised, at least in part, to prioritise the best interests of the whole organisation. Furthermore, those incentives have to feel as immediate as do the backyard ones, otherwise they still won't work.

Turning to lower down the organisational tree, Barack Obama's second book, *Audacity of Hope,* in the chapter on Faith, talks about the spectacular success of the non-denominational evangelical churches while the mainline Protestant churches are losing membership rapidly. He explains it in this way: "... their success ... points to a hunger that goes beyond any particular issue or cause. Each day, it seems, thousands of Americans ... are deciding that their work, their possessions, their diversions, their sheer busyness are not enough. They want a sense of purpose, a narrative arc to their lives, something that will relieve a chronic loneliness or lift them above the exhausting, relentless toil of daily life. They need an assurance that somebody out there cares about them, is listening to them – that they are not just destined to travel down a long highway towards nothingness." Now the mainline churches could be providing this assurance, so why aren't they? I suggest it is a communication failure on two fronts; they are not reaching out in the language of the people who need them, and their image is that of previous generations. In a way this is inevitable because an organisation cannot truly be all things to all people. So a long established, trusted organisation whose values are rooted in history and tradition has difficulty addressing the needs of people who have a 'here and now' focus. We can readily translate this communication challenge, and Obama's explanation of individual perceptions, into organisations.

Conflict can be a driver for progress, although not always what we planned or wanted. At the level of country conflict, war is often cited as a driver for technology progress. Richard Feynman in his books on the history of science continually refers back to WWII as the springboard for scientific breakthroughs. Part of the reason there is simple; the government spent a lot of money on research. The rest of the reason is a mix of patriotism, priorities, and collaboration instead of competition. WWI gave us the submachine gun, and WWII gave us the nuclear bomb, so it's not all good. At an organisation level, conflict can be a focus for extra energy and innovation by positive-thinking, problem-solving individuals and teams. More often though it is a huge distraction and waste of time and energy. On balance it is definitely best avoided.

digression: feeding the world

According to the UN World Food Programme (2016), 11% of the world population (795 million) do not get enough food to be healthy and lead an active life, and in the 21st century that number is *increasing*. Yet there is enough food in the world. WFP calculates that US$3.2 billion is needed per year to reach all 66 million hungry school-age children. This amount is less than 0.005% of the World GDP. So why don't we just do it? Do we need to make feeding a profitable venture for society to prioritise it, which it does so well in the developed world? I can choose between 15 different types of rice and 8 different type of tinned tuna in my supermarket. Feeding the undeveloped world is the challenge – how to make that profitable? Or what other incentives can we use instead of profit?

priorities

It is most common for individuals and groups to have a range of potential actions and a variety of incentives – a regular matrix of possibilities. So how do they prioritise, and how can we adjust the priorities to good effect?

We looked at Maslow's 'hierarchy of needs' in the previous section, and these can be summarised into the following priorities:

- First drive - biological: breathe, drink, eat, breed
- Second drive - interactive: reward & punishment to affect performance

- Third drive - intrinsic: rewards of enjoyment, fulfilment, recognition

In the context of an organisation and its staff, we can leave aside the first drive ... except for the drinking and eating. My observation is that staff do value an office building with high-quality kitchen and rest area facilities, and an organisation with a generous attitude towards providing food and drink and the time to enjoy it. However there are a lot of the first drive things that go on outside the work environment, and the relative quality of them is not generally a top priority in choosing to work for a particular organisation, or indeed choosing to work more productively.

You would imagine that a top priority for the second drive would be money. A variety of research has shown that whilst that is true for mechanical tasks, money as an incentive for performance in cognitive tasks simply does not work. It can even have a negative effect. What we need to do, it seems, is to pay people enough so that money is not an issue, and then provide them with autonomy, mastery and purpose. These 3 factors lead to better performance & personal satisfaction:

- Autonomy: desire to be self-directed, have some freedom, take responsibility
- Mastery: urge to get better at stuff, have more certainty, make a contribution
- Purpose: understanding of rationale and bigger picture, sense of right-ness

This is cogently and forcefully argued by Daniel Pink in his book *Drive: The Surprising Truth About What Motivates Us* and the book is nicely summarised in an animation of his talk at the RSA (see References).

---

illustration: why rich people keep working

By 'rich people' I mean those who already have more money than they can spend on themselves. Certainly some are philanthropists, happy to pay taxes to help their country's infrastructure and those less fortunate than themselves, and dispensing money to causes they believe in. Have a look at the Giving Pledge started by Gates and Buffett. When they are still in business while being philanthropists (for we are not talking the charity or public sector here), I suspect it is not so much what the money can buy, it's more the amount of money which is an indicator of power and status.

As to why they stay in business, the many interviews and articles online and in magazines such as Forbes suggest a number of reasons: they really enjoy the work; they are pathologically insecure; they cannot imagine doing anything else, or worse still doing nothing; they got there by working long and hard, and that is how they are wired up. The incentives that work for them are power and achievement.

A word of warning: watch out for the boss who does not need to work – their incentives can be hard to understand and anticipate. Certainly some will still act like conventional bosses, but others (and I had one once) are there to have fun by controlling people and playing games, and that can get very frustrating and messy.

Thinking still about the second drive, the law is an incentive, but a pretty negative one. Peer group pressure is another in the negative range. The positives are all about us feeling good, which could be physical safety and comfort, mental comfort (that beloved marketing phrase "peace of mind"), self-esteem, and respect from others. These latter positives stray up into the third level, where recognition is a powerful incentive for some. This takes many forms. For some a simple 'thank you' will suffice. For others it is promotion that proves their worth. Others again are focused on public accolades. When the desire for recognition is out of balance with individual and collective morals and scruples, this often leads to bad practices.

mindset

The mindsets of individuals, and the pressure on their thinking by their colleagues and bosses, can influence their incentives and priorities. Expectations can be reduced by bad experiences or by a general malaise in the organisation. A large part of the challenge for management, and for the change manager in particular, is to create and encourage a positive mindset.

There is a body of research that has looked at the differences between people who have a 'fixed' mindset and those with a 'growth' mindset:

- fixed mindset believes intelligence and ability is innate and unchangeable
- growth mindset believes that practice trumps talent, or rather increases talent

Carol Dweck is a leading psychologist at Stanford, and back in the 1970s she demonstrated that young people with a growth mindset fared much better when faced with new challenges than those with the fixed mindset. She went on in the 1990s to show that praising children for their intelligence, rather than for their effort, often leads them to give up when they encounter setbacks. These results have not always been reproducible, and Dweck herself accepts that the growth mindset is not a panacea, and there are many complicating factors – we are dealing with humans, after all.

Matthew Syed in his book *Bounce: the Myth of Talent and the Power of Practice* makes a compelling case for the advantages of the 'growth mindset' over the 'fixed mindset'. This may explain the attraction of top-performing athletes giving incentivising after-dinner speeches to business people; it is simply down to believing in yourself, learning from failures, knowing you can be better, and practicing like hell. In summary Syed says that an ethos constructed upon the potential for personal transformation is the underlying psychological principle driving high performance. A corollary of this is that businesses are much better off if they believe in and cultivate their staff and promote from within; those who habitually recruit external talent are fostering the 'fixed mindset' which saddles them with uneven, or worse still transitory, successes that fail to deliver a sustainable upward path.

localness

One way people prioritise their actions is according to their feeling of connection, of localness, to the issue or opportunity.

Identification with and incentive towards a problem diminishes with distance. There is a woman in an African country subsumed with grief at the death of her child ... and it's happening now ... and ... now ... and ... now. Do those outside that country all stand up and say we must do something about that and take concerted action? No. We may feel something, some frustration and even outrage when it is brought to our attention, and we may give some money to charity or even sign a petition or email our government. The people in that woman's family and probably in her village are very incentivised to act because they witness, they experience the distress and they know the context and the back story. Yet they don't have the means to stop it happening. The people in that area and in that country have less immediacy because they don't know the woman yet they may relate to the circumstances – they are the best bet for appropriate incentivised action. Those outside that country, outside that continent, are much less incentivised to act because that woman is one of many statistics, they have a lesser understanding of the situation, and they have problems enough of their own.

Campaigns for action across a large group of people are successful when they manage to make it feel local to the individuals. Also, frankly, it helps when the campaign organisers make it easy to participate in a meaningful way and give plenty of feedback on progress.

If we look at the number of charities that exist, there are far more than the number of issues they address, and one could also argue that some of the issues are more appropriate for government than charity. In the UK there are over 160,000 registered charities plus countless tiny ones not required to be registered. The interesting question here is why those charities with very similar aims exist and are continuing to be formed? Why is this happening now when it didn't happen in previous societies? What are the incentives? It's about both the instigators and those who contribute, about having a personal connection and operating on a local scale. A human scale you might say. Or a trusted scale. People feel compelled to 'do something' when they have lost a loved one in unnatural circumstances, be it accident, war, medical mistake, or currently incurable disease. Did they always? What happened 25, 50, 100 years ago before we had the capability, before such a thing was made practical by the communication revolution? Now it is all too easy, and one wonders how effective all those small actions are? They are effective for the instigators because they feel they are achieving something - it may be hard but it's very direct and immediate. They have in some sense regained the control that they felt had been lost.

Michael Lewis in *The Big Short* recounts the financial crisis of 2008 within the USA, and how a number of contrarian, or perhaps simply unblinkered, investors made a whole lot of money. The incentives across the investment community might be thought to be making money and nothing else. Yet some people were doing it just because they could, either for recognition within their peer group or purely for their own self-satisfaction. Whilst they needed to understand the big picture to be successful, they measured their success in a local way, against a small band of similar professional investors, and against their standing in their community.

People are different

Change is something we may do, or it may be done to us – we may be an instigator, manager, participant or recipient. How we manage or deal with a change depends on the role we have, and the type of person we are. Management is not all about top-down, proactive direction; sometimes upward, reactive management is called for, usually when there has been poor planning, consultation and communication.

So don't think of change management as only a specific skill-set for change managers, it is more about a set of principles and skills around comprehensive planning (in the broadest sense) and communication (not just one-way).

Here we'll discuss a few differences in people types that help in understanding interpersonal dynamics within teams and between management levels. In the following segment titles I don't mean them to be combative – it just seems appropriate to draw distinctions between two opposites.

nature v. nurture

People are wired up in a variety of ways, and their first 20 years or so in family and education can reinforce or indeed suppress their natural tendencies. We all know people who are naturally cautious, others who are adventurous, some who are straight-line thinkers, others who are lateral thinkers, and so on.

Equally people can alter or evolve, to some extent, the way they think about things and interact with others in the work context, usually through a combination of learning and experience. People can change a bit, through increased self-awareness and removal of stress, but rarely by much in a sustained way. We are very unlikely to sustainably change them through external pressure, and such an attempt can have the reverse results to those intended. They can change themselves with a combination of understanding and incentive. This does not typically happen within the timeframe of a single change project.

In summary, seek to understand your team members and work with what you have. Focus on their strengths and avoid their weaknesses. It helps to be honest about your own strengths and weaknesses too, as long as you do not undermine your authority or respect in so doing.

horizontal v. vertical

People are generally good at handling either breadth of responsibility or depth of responsibility. In other words a wide range of high-level responsibility, or responsibility for something specific that goes from strategy down to the dirty detail. Combining the two usually kills them, whether they acknowledge this or not. There are always rare exceptions, on both ends of the spectrum.

In large programmes the timescales and complexities of the deliverables are usually much bigger than that to which one person can comfortably relate. Where there is considerable intellectual and emotional baggage that has built up over many years, the effect is worsened. The horizontal people (and I don't mean laid back) are more comfortable and effective working across large swathes of the programme and relying upon others for the detail, whereas vertical people are more comfortable and effective with a narrow scope that goes down into detail.

Where we have staff who are long-service, and are subject matter experts, this is an advantage in analysing and understanding the nature and mechanism of implementing the change. Paradoxically it is also a weakness because these people are able, and only too willing, to talk about many parts of the programme and offer informed opinions without reference to documentation. These opinions, naturally, are rooted in the past – that which they know – rather than the future – that which they may fear, deny, or dismiss. The trick is to use the advantage of experience whilst avoiding those weaknesses, through very strong discipline on the ownership of deliverables and issue resolution, and very strong clarity on who leads and who supports.

I think it matters less what kind of person an individual is, and more what incentivises them. Of course there is a cross-over, in that a risk-taker could be assumed to be incentivised by unknowns. But a risk-taker may be incentivised towards a known and comfortable state and they are simply prepared to take a riskier approach to get there than the cautious profile – the same outcome is intended, and we may or may not get there more quickly!

facilitating v. directing

Horatio Nelson's approach to life and battles is often over-simplified as "go straight at 'em". This does not entirely do justice to his strategic abilities, at least before battles. In summing up Nelson's life, Roger Knight in *The Pursuit of Victory* includes the following observations which are entirely relevant within a modern day organisation:

- he had a reputation for coolness under fire, and there are dozens of examples of his physical courage - he had luck too, many times over, sometimes turning on a moment

- decisions made in the quiet of his cabin were often more difficult than the instinctive brilliance he displayed at the height of battle
- those who command can be divided into those that control and those that delegate; the minority who can bring themselves to trust subordinates reap the greater rewards - despite his concern for detail, Nelson was very much in the latter camp
- men follow and are attracted to those who represent certainty, especially in situations that are confusing, dangerous and fast-moving; but in more subtle situations (such as the political intrigue in Naples and his infatuation with Emma Hamilton), certainty can become liability

Nelson, then, was certainly a 'directing' type of person, supremely self-confident especially under pressure, and a highly calculated risk-taker who led from the front. Sometimes organisations, and change programmes, need that single person with ultimate power to create an energy and focus, to rally people and carry them forward.

Only a minority of people are naturally in this mould, though many others can rise to the occasion when required. If we can direct confidently and forcefully whilst also delegating and listening to others, then all will be well. What we don't want to do is close our eyes and ears, and cross over the line into being a dictator. I suggest that, when the need arises, we can become that 'directing' person by focusing on one top-priority issue at a time.

The 'facilitating' person is very different role, where we are we are typically one of many people in a position of some power, and often we are helping those more powerful than ourselves. I am going to spend a bit more time on this, simply because I believe that everyone can be a facilitator and it is a very useful technique.

Facilitation is a skill that has many components. The most important of all is self-awareness. This means knowing our own flaws, limitations, even preferences, and watching out for them getting in the way. It also means observing how we are affecting other people by what we say, our body language, even how we dress.

After that comes the ability to be aware of others, to read their body language and hear the real messages behind their words, or the lack of them. These components underpin our ability to say the right thing in the right way at the right time, that has a positive effect on the listeners and translates into their attitudes and actions that bear positively on the situation.

So putting that together we are most effective if the people we are facilitating have a trust in us. That trust is established by showing an empathy for their position – showing we understand, using their language rather than ours, and having a non-judgemental attitude.

In our own actions it is important to be selective, to show good intent, to be confident in our approach, to be clear in what we mean, and to emphasise we don't have all the answers and might even be wrong occasionally. All of these things will enhance the trust in our relationship, and as observed elsewhere, trust can move mountains.

Finally a healthy dose of pragmatism and good humour almost always oils the wheels.

Now you might be saying "I can't be all those things – and I certainly can't be thinking about them whilst have a deep conversation about a complex problem". True. No-one said it is easy. Practice is a wonderful thing though, and start gently, not expecting too much of yourself the first few times. Try to bite off what you feel you can chew, and you will be surprised at how the size of the bites will grow. Facilitation is a skill and whilst some people are naturally more adept at it, almost everyone can learn the skill through thinking and practice; and it is good for you too, and you do not need to ace every component to be a decent facilitator.

A good way to improve is to make a list of the skill components and then ask someone you know well to rate you on each one. Ideally you do this with a non-work friend and a work colleague, though not one in your current immediate circle where you are needing to provide some facilitation. It might be interesting to see if there is a different perception in the two different environments. Keep in mind though that this is perception, it's a subjective assessment by two different people so use it as an indicator rather than treating it as the black and white truth.

digression: dog or cat

In 2013 the mobile operator O2 started an advertising campaign in the UK with the tag line "be more dog: to dogs, life is one big adventure - they never stop playing and exploring." O2 had the temerity to show a cat doing dog-like things, and I'm still unsure of the point of that, though clearly they want O2 customers to never stop playing and exploring so that they pay for more minutes and data. To generalise, I suggest that dogs are undiscerning; they love anyone that loves them, and they get excited at the same thing every time. If you are owned by a cat you will recognise that cats are very good at filtering information; I have no idea if they do it consciously or unconsciously, though they certainly do it when apparently sleeping. They don't twitch an ear at a loud noise or a movement with which they are familiar, yet they jump at a new noise that is so quiet we cannot hear it or at a tiny movement that is unexpected. **I suggest we should seek to be more cat.**

Trust is golden

It often takes a long time to establish trust, yet it can be lost in an ill-judged moment. Trust is a very personal assessment, an ephemeral thing, yet hugely powerful. It is a large factor in how we humans successfully cooperate in groups.

Trust can be between individuals, groups of people (departments, projects), or whole organisations.

We have already referred to trust and what it does in a variety of situations in this chapter. Let's now discuss trust itself.

what is trust?

What is it really? Is it a black and white thing, or are there shades of grey?

I do not expect someone I trust to be perfect. If I trust someone it means I have tangible evidence that they are capable, honest, open and loyal. To unpick that a little further, it means that I can predict their capabilities, actions and reactions, that they are aligned and complementary with mine, and also that I can rely on them to communicate well.

I have friends and colleagues that I trust in some situations and not in others. For instance someone at work may be hugely practical and a great problem-solver yet be completely hopeless in writing things down for the benefit of others. That does not mean I don't trust that person, it means I know where and when to trust them and when they need support.

It follows that if there is a specific task to be done, I trust one person a bit more than another to get it done. We should be able to justify whether or not we trust someone or not in a given situation; justifying how much we trust that person in general becomes subjective and difficult and discussing it risks generating confusion and disappointment.

So to answer my earlier question, it is black and white for a given person in a given situation, although it is far from black and white for each person.

As to the question "what is it really" I provide this very broad suggestion: it is being comfortable in putting your own success in the hands of someone else.

Think of any aspect of your life where you are doing something new; are you not more comfortable, more relaxed if you know what to expect, if you are confident it is the right thing, if the outcome is reasonably predictable? In other words, if you trust the situation, the people involved, and indeed your own judgement? If you have certainty?

It is no different in organisations, in fact it's even more so. People are usually nervous about changes, for a whole raft of reasons – a lot of it is uncertainty, born out of a lack of understanding about the what, why, where, when, who and how of the change.

There is a virtuous circle to be had here: if we reduce uncertainty, through some clear and appropriate communication, then we build trust; and if we build trust, through showing and sharing understanding, then we reduce uncertainty. It is a matter of communication, which includes tone of voice and body language (or written style and imagery) as well as the content of what is said.

If we have trust in a person or a situation:

- we have less uncertainty
- we need less communication or direction
- we are more confident of the right outcomes

how to establish and maintain trust

Trust must be actively maintained; without reinforcement it fades in respect of situations or organisations, because they alter and evolve. This is less so with individual people as, despite many claims by many self-help schemes, people generally do not alter very much, for good or bad. That is my experience.

Here are some of the ways of establishing trust between people, individuals or groups:

- find common ground, common interests or concerns
- adapt our language and terminology to that of others
- encourage two-way communications at all times
- adapt to people's styles or preferences in communication and management
- deliver on small commitments, be consistent

Maintain trust using the following, in addition to continuing with the above list:

- be proactive, anticipate needs
- be the change (act as you wish others to act)
- be honest and find the positives
- if breaking a promise, do it early, deliver something, and make a new promise
- remember, we can lose it in a moment

secondary trust

There are times when we have to work with or request action from people or organisations with whom we have no direct experience, no established trust. Our best approach then is get a recommendation and introduction from someone that we do trust. In my terms we have a primary trust with the latter, and through them we establish a secondary trust with the new party.

This secondary trust works both ways, of course, because the new party will be more open and positive about our approach than if we were going to them completely cold.

A simple personal example is when I need a plumber in my house for the first time. Do I look in the local paper and pick someone at random, relying on my ability to assess them when they arrive? This is high risk because I'm not a plumber (otherwise I would not need one) and I'm unlikely to assess him or her until after the work is done, and the consequences of a bad plumbing job can be anything from irritating to downright disastrous. I don't like that risk. How much better to ask a few neighbours and find a recommendation that gives me some confidence in the plumber's attitude, timeliness and previous work. There is also the option of going online to one of the many 'trusted trader' websites, and that might help in the absence of neighbours, although it's a little bit too secondary for my liking – I'm not sure that I trust the website. I much prefer a personal conversation with a 'recommender' because I can ask specific questions, and I know the plumber knows that I have done this.

This all translates into change management in organisations of course, and I'm sure you can see how, so I will just make the general point about introductions. Change often requires new people, on a temporary or permanent basis, and typically they are needed to be productive very quickly. The risk of hiring the wrong people is significantly reduced if the candidates are already known or recommended, because their CV is bolstered by personal assessment and recommendation. This applies equally to selecting new suppliers or partners for the organisation.

Nothing beats people you have worked with before, however when they are not available this secondary trust model is very valuable.

failure can be good

Counter-intuitive though it may seem, I believe that failures can be a part of selecting, and establishing trust with, new colleagues. This is particularly true if they do not come with a recommendation or secondary trust attached. Looking back at the story at the beginning of the chapter, we might imagine that Tom has developed a degree of trust in Elena, because she delivered what was requested and managed her situation well. On the other hand, Chas may feel let down by Tom because he didn't test the business model early enough, and would have trouble trusting him in another adventure.

That's not to say we must *only* work on trust and ignore the due diligence, governance structure, planning & reporting methodology, risk analysis, and so on when running a change programme – perish the thought. At some point, though, the organisation, specifically the sponsoring or accountable senior manager, has to be able to trust the people doing this good work, that they are doing it right. We could instead have three teams doing the same work in parallel and compare results. That is probably overkill, except perhaps for space exploration (or ocean exploration aka deep sea drilling) where there is so much to lose from a small mistake (although I believe IBM used to do it in their early software development).

So where does Failure come in? It is a well-established view that the most successful entrepreneurs are those with a failure or two under their belts – failure can teach someone a lot if they are prepared to embrace it, and it toughens them up - in a good way. (Either that or they stop being an entrepreneur altogether, because it was the wrong choice for them.) I suggest that this applies equally to the field of change management.

We need to assess this potential new colleague, or supplier or partner organisation ... can we trust them? Naturally the individual, or representative, is going to focus on their successes. My contention is that we can put more trust in the person who openly and honestly discusses a failure or two, compared to the person who has apparently only ever been a brilliant success. (The person who admits to a majority of failures should be gently shown the door, and given the telephone number of the nearest career-change office.) A discussion of what a person has learned from their failures, or partial successes, can be illuminating. It is not necessarily the nature of the failure, but how they dealt with it and how they talk about their approach to avoiding similar problems in future that can generate the trust we need.

Hearts & minds

Winning hearts and minds originated as an idea of persuading your enemies, instead of defeating them by force. Whilst I'm not suggesting that certain people within an organisation are treated as enemies, the principle of persuasion over coercion is important.

If we win the hearts and minds, the actions will follow. To put it another way, if people want something to happen then they will find a way. The reverse is all too painfully true.

The Survey On Change by Impact Executives referenced in Chapter 1 reports that two-thirds of respondents believe that 'passion' is the most important element in delivering a change project, compared with one-third who believe it is 'process'. I think in broad terms that we can equate 'passion' with 'hearts and minds'.

resistance

Not all resistance is futile, despite what they say in films - some is well-founded. Where there is a clear negative impact on individuals, the challenge is to handle that early, honestly, and constructively, and finding or creating whatever positives we can to protect dignity and self-respect.

Unfounded resistance very often comes from fear, or misjudgement born out of ignorance.

fear and ignorance

Most of us are uncomfortable when faced with unknowns that affect us, and depending on the size & nature of the effect we may be fearful. "Will I still have a job next month" is an unknown that usually makes us fear for our income and our self-respect. Fearful people can act irrationally, and fear tends to spread: it is best avoided.

Fear arising from the danger of mental or physical injury or death is perfectly understandable and deep-rooted – however we are hopefully not dealing with that in change management. Fear of change usually arises from ignorance, and can be mitigated or even avoided by timely consultation and communication. Perhaps the job is truly at risk, in which case explain the factors involved, the decision process, even the redundancy & support package.

You can have the best idea for a change to improve something, and you can implement it to prove it works, and still it will not be recognised for what it is if you have not taken people with you, if you or they are ignorant of the intentions. Richard P Feynman was one of the world's greatest theoretical physicists in the 20th century and a winner of the Nobel Prize for Physics. His mixture of high intelligence, unquenchable curiosity, eternal scepticism and his complete inability to give up on an unsolved problem got him into scrapes whilst still a boy, as he describes in his book *Surely You're Joking Mr. Feynman!*. He was working as a desk clerk for his aunt who ran a hotel, and he adapted the telephone switchboard so that it was quicker to answer a call if he wasn't behind the desk, such as setting up card tables or sitting on the front porch. It only consisted of moving the mouthpiece and tying threads to the toggles. It worked well for him, but his aunt got cross when she came to do a stint at the desk. She didn't set up card tables and didn't want to sit on the porch, so she didn't perceive the problem he was solving. Young Feynman for his part only saw the effectiveness of the solution and probably did not appreciate the negative aesthetics of having threads and the mouthpiece on view to guests.

Later in his life Professor Feynman tried and succeeded in all sorts of activities (e.g. languages, drumming, safe-cracking) because despite his self-acknowledged ignorance when he came across them he was fearless … and very, very smart. At the end of the book he makes a hugely important point that science must always acknowledge all the factors and report all the results, not just the ones that support the expected or desired result. Wilful ignorance causes distortions and errors, and the same is true when managing change – don't ignore the inconvenient.

overcoming distrust

Back in the 1990s I advised a small, fragmented organisation (let's call it the Institution) on their move towards an integrated communications infrastructure. The rest of this segment is my paper presented to the Board at the time, which provides a useful analysis of the eternal hearts & minds challenge.

Introduction

This is a short paper of observations and suggestions on the Institution's organisation and dynamics, in relation to the successful implementation of voice and data networking. As the Institution is no doubt aware, it is essential to consider the staff attitudes and incentives when looking at a sizeable project, especially one which focuses on inter-communication. The following are probably statements of the obvious, yet sometimes it is useful to have the obvious written down.

The Current State

There is something of a chasm between the Computing department and the rest of the Institution. This is by no means unusual in companies and organisations, but it is always a serious concern. Rightly or wrongly, the Computer facilities have a poor reputation. Staff have low expectations and a high degree of cynicism concerning the provision of what they see as necessary to the business.

The Required State ...

To be successful in implementing any part of a communications system, it is essential that all appropriate staff are involved and participating. This will require a turn-around in attitudes, which is not an easy task.

Staff need to understand what is happening and why, and equally importantly what is not happening and why not. They must be trained so that they have self-belief and confidence. They must give their commitment, willingly, to making the project succeed.

... and How to Get There

Reliability is everything. If the Institution commits to doing something, and it works on time and continues to work all the time, then attitudes will change and will do so quite quickly.

Staff expectations should be suitably channelled with decisive direction from the top and achievable goals. Small 'wins' should be planned, to build confidence; predictable delivery of simple, obvious benefits will ensure that staff use the facilities to good effect. This in turn will improve confidence for the next goals, generating a 'virtuous circle'.

An 'awayday' for relevant staff is very useful for achieving common understanding, a genuine sense of participation, and commitment (the 'sign-up'). It is important that this be off-site, to give credibility to the session and to ensure concentration.

It follows that the Institution should only implement what it knows it can manage, only provide facilities that will be 100% reliable in the services they provide. Thus the priorities and speed of implementation must be moderated by the skills and experience available, both to implement and to support.

I could write much the same paper today around the principles of repairing trust. Chasms still exist in many organisations between IT and the business, between research and operations, between product development and sales. Wherever there are differing local incentives, the battle for hearts & minds must be engaged.

tools and techniques

Let me offer a number of loosely connected observations and suggestions to wrap up this section and indeed the chapter.

Change the mantra of "we can't do that because" to "we can do this instead". Turning negatives into positives can seem a bit like trickery, yet presented in a professional way it can be very effective in creating a more engaged mindset.

Talk about the positives all the time, not as a hard sell but as a constant context. People buy in to success.

To repurpose John F Kennedy's famous rhetoric: ask not "how do I want to deliver it", but instead ask "how would I want it delivered to me".

Don't expect to be liked by everyone. Do ensure that through honesty, predictability, innovation and sharing that we are understood and respected by everyone.

A brand for a change programme is useful to maintain a focus over a long period and/or across a wide selection of stakeholders, i.e. anyone who is likely to be affected by the change. More than a name or logo, which is useful in itself for visual identification, this includes an attitude, ethos, and values.

Humour is a great facilitator when used sensitively and sparingly.

Help people to feel a part of what is going on by giving them a small role, even if it is invented, or some insider glimpse – this improves their sense of belonging and increases the likelihood of them being a supporter.

Above all, if we put ourselves in the position of each of our stakeholders, and do our best to look at the change from their point of view, then we stand the best chance of understanding and influencing their incentives.

Takeaways

- there is conscious or unconscious self-interest in everyone's actions
- we tend towards optimism in making change, and pessimism in receiving change
- the single common factor across changes within all organisations and societies is people
- understanding and modifying people's incentives is the key to effective management
- autonomy, mastery & purpose mean more than money in cognitive tasks
- local factors drive action more than regional or global factors
- people are wired up in different ways – understand this and use it, don't abuse it
- trust means being comfortable in putting our own success in the hands of someone else
- establishing and maintaining trust is the best amplifier for action
- trust can be lost in an ill-judged moment, and takes weeks or months to repair
- ignorance breeds fear which encourages resistance
- known problems are preferable to uncertainty
- always talk about the positives because people buy into success

3 Start at the End

Monday: Finally the 0930 meeting starts at 1015, once Pietro, the Food Safety Director, has torn himself away from the operational crises of the morning. The Sponsor introduces Simon, saying he is an interim change manager and here to help the department with their urgent programme of work to satisfy the regulatory Inspector. Simon starts to explain his standard list, including vision statement, list of outcomes, measurable benefits, and asks where documents can be found. Pietro interrupts agitatedly "we haven't got time for all that, we need a database and we've got to hire 4 people now - we promised the Regulator that we'd deliver an analysis of the data by the end of the month." Simon realises of course that they mean the current month, and today is the 10th already. He decides to push the meeting hard for a decent review of the strategic and tactical outcomes before getting into the planning. It is now or never to get this right.

Tuesday 0900: the boardroom is packed with whiteboards, flipcharts and 15 reluctant people. Simon has negotiated permission to use this room in order to make a subliminal statement about the importance of the workshop. "Right" says Simon, calling the meeting to order, "the plan in the next 6 hours is to capture the deliverables that we need, in order to achieve these outcomes signed off by the Sponsor yesterday, and then identify the dependencies between them, using non-technical language." "But what's the point" comes a voice from the other end of the room, "we've got an impossible deadline, we know what we need and we must get started. We've got to show the Inspector some progress." Shufflings and mutterings around the room suggest this is a consensus view. Simon draws a deep breath "look, we've been given this time today by the Sponsor and Pietro, and I honestly think it will be helpful, especially as we have all the subject matter experts in the room, so please let's give it a try".

Five and a half hours later they look at the whiteboards and flipcharts filled with writing in a rainbow of colours and swooping lines connecting items like a crazy spider's web. "Uh, this is huge" says the original dissenter "I thought we only had to fix the data and write a report". "Yeah, and I see a problem" says Jayesh, "I wasn't going to start for 2 weeks, I'm kinda busy right now, but it looks like everyone else is dependent on my deliverables – I'll have to change my priorities".

"I know we're all knackered" says Simon with an encouraging smile "however there's one more question I'd like us to tackle for everyone's benefit. Is this" he says as he waves his hand towards the walls "all you want from the programme, or is there the opportunity along the way to solve a few other challenges as well? Are there other current issues that if not included will mean these outcomes are not sustainable?" The bodies that had been in various slumped positions sat forward again ... you could hear the brains re-engaging.

Wednesday 1000: Simon meets with Pietro, Helen the Research Manager, and Mary the Quality Manager. "Yesterday's workshop was very productive, and here's the list of deliverables grouped by the outcome they support." Simon distributes an A3 sheet around the table. "What also became clear" he continues, following up with an A4 sheet "is this short list of additional things to fix at the same time; including these in the programme will avoid almost immediate re-work. I blocked people's pet projects by ensuring the whole workshop agreed on the priority of each item." "No, no" cry Pietro and Helen at the same time "it's too risky, too complicated, we don't have time." Simon waits a couple of heartbeats before placing his counter argument "the current promises to the Inspector were made in good faith but we can see now they are simply unachievable. We have to re-negotiate, so let's do it with a positive story." The debate continues around whether the Inspector is an enemy or an expert friend, and Helen concedes the Inspector is interested in us succeeding rather than failing. Mary then quietly suggests that she and Simon take the additional list to the Sponsor.

Thursday 1300: Simon meets with Pietro, Helen and Mary again. "Thanks for meeting again at such short notice. The Sponsor has agreed the broader set of outcomes, depending on the timeline and risk matrix, and on an early meeting with the Inspector to get their sign-up." Pietro leans forward "so what's the new delivery date?" "I have no idea yet!" responds Simon "We just have an agreed set of outcomes supported by a list of deliverables – now we have to work back and create an achievable plan." "Ok," says Helen "I get that, so let's write to the Inspector now explaining what we're doing and promising phased, verifiable improvements and a timeline for that within say 2 weeks". Simon smiles, thinking that things were going the right way now "and the next step here is to get the right people involved in doing the detailed planning" he says.

Friday 1400: Simon meets with the five people who have been assigned by their bosses to have project manager responsibility; most of them are subject matter experts or operational people with no experience in organising and running a project. Simon lays out the programme structure, grouping activities into projects where each project can realistically be the responsibility of one person.

Jayesh stabs at the flipchart "this is great, if we hadn't included all this it would have been a messy temporary fix." "Ok" says Alan getting up, "now I can see how my project fits into the whole picture, so I'll get going and let you know when I'm done." Simon winces. "Alan, it's still not quite that simple. We have to estimate how long each task will take, and the resources needed, and plug that all into a plan that has acceptable levels of risk." As Alan sinks back deflated, Simon continues "but look on the bright side ... you'll be able to schedule your other work with confidence, and you'll know you have the resources you need instead of scrapping for them every Monday morning!"

The previous chapters have been laying the ground, setting up the context, and providing general commentary for my approaches to managing change. From here in I am providing more focused and directed observations and advice, on the various aspects of how to deal with change, how to manage change, how to get the best out of change – all with the emphasis on the people and what drives them. In this chapter we talk about how to start, and specifically where to start.

The story above is a painful illustration of the pressures when an organisation is panicked by external demands. It looks as though they have little experience of organising a large plan of work. Their first reaction is to just get started in what seems the right sort of direction, and hope.

My father had a favourite phrase when faced with the need to make a plan for the day with the family: "let's work back" he would say, meaning let's identify the fixed end-point – for example my bedtime, my need to do school homework, my commitment to meet friends in the pub (you can see me getting older there). Then he would list the contents of the day, estimate the time for the fixed ones (driving to the beach) and adjust the time for the flexible ones (sailing the boat). Occasionally the analysis would show that we should have left an hour ago, and then some radical re-planning was required (homework was ring-fenced, but bedtime and pubtime could be negotiated). My daughters have now taken up the family chant "let's work back". It is obvious, isn't it?

There is a positive flow to setting up a change, in terms of doing things in the right order. If we start in the wrong place then sooner or later we will be swimming upstream which is very hard work – ask a salmon. If we haven't agreed a clear, achievable outcome then we might swim up the wrong river altogether. If we don't know what to measure, and how to measure it, we won't know when we have reached the right part of the right river. If we get the governance structure wrong then sooner or later we will be attempting to climb a waterfall, with the attendant danger of drowning.

Forward in the fog

How often do we start out making a change with too little information, too little confidence, and a feeling that our plans are optimistic, driven by statements of desire? If we think they *might* be optimistic, the chances are that they are *very* optimistic. It is a fact of life that if things can go wrong, they almost certainly will go wrong, and most changes take longer and/or cost more than anticipated.

how far can we see?

Let's examine that last observation: what do we mean by anticipated, and what is the quality of that anticipation. Here we need to draw a distinction between a task that has been done many times before under very similar circumstances, and all the other tasks that have some or many elements of newness. The 'repeat' tasks really can be well anticipated, so that all the possible problems have been pre-handled; this is a rare situation in change management – in fact it is rare in life. In non 'repeat' tasks, critical thinking is essential at every step.

It may be helpful to distinguish between Mandatory change (typically external, such as regulatory or legal, and often with demanding deadlines) versus Discretionary change (where the decision is made within the organisation). Whilst both need the same treatment and the same components, it is tempting with mandatory change to say "we have got to do it, so let's get started on the first steps – we'll feel better when we have done something". Nevertheless even regulation-driven change is negotiable to some extent, and deadlines do move. It is still important to work out where we need to be, and by when.

There will be occasional situations where we genuinely cannot define the outcome until we have started the work. Perhaps the best we can do is to scrupulously examine the rationales for changing away from the current status quo, to elicit some clues as to acceptable outcomes, or even just optimal directions in which to start. In such a case, do not promise anything about the eventual outcomes, do not even try to define them. Instead, depending on the practicalities, either embark upon a pilot or test project, or conduct a thought experiment. In this way we test the thinking and try out different approaches or routes, until we can formulate an achievable and acceptable set of outcomes. Then we go back and start again with our change, with that experience under our belt.

illustration: creating a nearer end

In the entrepreneurial context it can be hard to predict or even define the end goal other than untold riches and worldwide fame. The autobiography shelves are littered with successful people who 'just went out and did it'. That deceptively simple recipe hides the fact that many more people went out and failed, due to lack of planning and controls, and those people don't write autobiographies.

A friend of mine, long ago, had an idea for an online video delivery service. He had no idea how well this would be received or what revenue it could generate, or indeed what it would cost to set up. So naturally the bank and various angel investor funding channels were not interested in providing any start-up funds. So he defined a 'nearer' end for his project, of building a mock-up and obtaining 100 commitments to use the service when available as demonstrated. This first project was funded by family & friends, who at least trusted him to do his best and not waste the money, even if they were lukewarm about the service.

He completed this project by working back from what would be needed to obtain those commitments. This success ensured some angel investor funding to build the next stage, a functioning prototype which was his next 'nearer end' before going on to develop the whole service.

critical thinking and questioning

We identify in Chapter 2 that a sense of belonging is central to achieving a positive approach. One of the ways to achieve this is to have a clear, commonly shared understanding of the why, what, how, when and where ... and one of the ways to achieve *that* is through asking good questions. Questions can occur to us spontaneously, and they can be generated by applying some critical thinking. The latter usually generate a better result.

Critical thinking is not a matter of thinking up criticisms. It is a thinking process that avoids assumptions, applies experience, uses facts, analyses logically, and identifies uncertainty, risk, error and lack of clarity. It comes up with constructive questions that are designed to shed light, remove uncertainty, reduce risk, and correct error.

Critical thinking does not have to be a structured exercise taking hour or days. It can be done on the hoof whilst reading a document or in a meeting. In essence it is about being constructively analytical, rather than being emotional, reactive or manipulative.

Richard Paul and Linda Elder in *The Miniature Guide to Critical Thinking Concepts and Tools* define a well cultivated critical thinker in this way:

- gathers and assesses relevant information, using abstract ideas to interpret it effectively, comes to well-reasoned conclusions and solutions, testing them against relevant criteria and standards

- thinks open-mindedly within alternative systems of thought, recognising and assessing, as need be, their assumptions, implications, and practical consequences
- raises vital questions and problems, formulating them clearly and precisely
- communicates effectively with others in figuring out solutions to complex problems

What I mean above by a 'good' question is one that is relevant, should be answerable by the recipient, and should generate a useful answer. By comparison, a 'bad' question is one that is the opposite of any of those three attributes. The use of 'should' is important, because if for instance the recipient cannot answer a question when we would expect them to be able to do so, this has generated useful information albeit of a negative kind.

There is no such thing as a 'dumb question', although there are plenty of dumb ways of asking a question. We talk later about 'speaking for the listener' and elsewhere about not alienating people; both of these are crucial when asking questions. We need to achieve the balance of being assertive and penetrating without being destructive or critical.

Types of good questions include:

- questions that go beyond the apparent boundaries in order to challenge narrow or limited thinking and establish what those boundaries really are
- questions that stimulate a new line of thinking
- questions where we know the answer, but others in the room don't and will benefit from hearing it

Types of bad questions include:

- where the recipient will be embarrassed in front of others

- where the question is political or mischievous
- where the answer cannot be known at this stage

Dumb ways of asking questions include:

- giving our own version of the answer in the question
- delivering a personal or emotional context or justification for the question
- asking something that has just been asked, because we were not listening

---

digression: ask when we know the answer

At first sight this looks like we are trying to catch someone out, in which case it belongs in the 'bad questions' category. There are times, though, when this can be used constructively.

I was in a large programme meeting, about 30 people from all over the company, where the Operations Director addressed us on how the change they were delivering was going to be run operationally. This was good in giving a context for their work, yet I could sense from the body language around me a level of discomfort. The Ops Dir was blithely assuming everything would work perfectly, yet the team had been immersed for months in issues, risks and assumptions. I had been working on the beta test and the roll-back plans, and so knew there was a full understanding of the need for careful implementation with contingencies. So I asked the question when the chance came: "I understand your focus is on when the changes have all settled down – could you say something about how the transition will be managed, what we will do if there are problems when we go live?" I could have given a very full answer to my own question, of course, but the summary from the Ops Dir put the room's mind at ease.

The assumption may be that questions are always asked 'upwards' i.e. to those in greater authority and with broader knowledge. Asking 'sideways' to our peers and 'downwards' to more junior staff are equally valuable. Our peers have useful advice and insights even if they are not specifically involved. Junior staff may well be subject matter experts in their area and have detail and long history that we may need. Tom Gilb (www.gilb.com) includes these questions for non-technical executives to ask when faced with a 'yes/no' decision on a complex change:

- why isn't the improvement quantified
- what is the degree of the risk and uncertainty, and why
- where did you get that from, how can I check it out
- how do you know it works that way, did you do it before
- have we got a complete solution, are all objectives satisfied
- who is responsible for failure or success
- how can we be sure that the plan is working, early in the project

Often a part of the problem is the over-reliance on a numerical financial analysis and forecast (prediction might be a better word, or even clairvoyance). A spreadsheet business case looks very trustworthy and convincing due to the level of detail, and yet so often it is based upon huge assumptions, vague estimates, or our old friend 'statements of desire'. They are also prone to small, well-obscured errors that generate significantly wrong results. Of course the spreadsheet is a useful tool, but don't just believe the answer unless all the underlying parameters can be clearly validated and risk-assessed. Instead, use it as a tool for scenario testing, as discussed in the next segment.

Some people are great at selling poor ideas, others are poor at selling great ideas – guess who has the higher profile? If a proposed change is claimed to be a no-brainer, risk-free, with no down-side, then I advise an even closer critical scrutiny than normal.

rise above the fog

Analysis and assessment should always be on the broadest basis possible, involving experience as well as evidence, opinion as well as fact, prediction as well as prescription.

Beware of apparently incontrovertible facts stated with insufficient explanation or caveats. For instance, it is well known that water does not flow uphill – right? Wrong. In a narrow, smooth channel of sufficiently gentle gradient and with a strong enough wind behind it, the water *does* flow uphill. The statement should have said that water does not flow uphill of its own volition. We can and must question simple facts that are presented baldly.

Adam Kahane in his book *Transformative Scenario Planning: Working Together to Change the Future* covers change on a grand and complex scale, where there is a huge amount of uncertainty. He started on this road, in the 1990s, through becoming involved in the dismantling of apartheid in South Africa. This was a classic example of where the desired outcome is simple to state and yet the intended and unintended consequences of going there are huge and complex, as are the choices of route. The heart of his transformative scenario planning is the construction of stories to describe and illustrate each scenario. Through those stories the participants can explore consequences and actions. This is what we need to do if any of the following is true: desired outcome is poorly defined; desired outcome has high risk; desired outcome has uncertain consequences; the route to the outcome is unclear.

There is another approach within scenario planning, which is more relevant in a quantitative analysis where there are a number of uncertain parameters. A model is created, typically a spreadsheet, and then tested with ranges and combinations of parameter values, to see where it works and where it breaks.

Focus on outcomes

In the simplest terms, a change is all about getting from 'here' to 'there'. It helps a lot to have a good definition of what 'there' looks like, so that we will know when we have arrived.

Whilst I am not generally fond of cute phrases, because they are usually too neat and simple, I do like "Keep your Eyes on the Prize" because it summarises the whole discipline of defining the required outcome and benefits and then maintaining a clear and unwavering focus upon achieving them.

When building a new office block or a bridge, the engineering challenges can be immense, although the successful outcome is pretty simple to define, and there is a body of knowledge and expertise going back hundreds of years. It is not quite so easy when re-engineering an organisation's business processes or governance structure or IT systems. These latter are much less likely to be 'repeat' tasks that can directly replicate and wholly build upon previous examples, and the successful outcome is often much harder to define and measure.

In the case of blue-sky research we generally cannot define the outcome at all, and there may be unforeseen benefits. Nevertheless, there has to be a reason for embarking on even a blue-sky route, and that reason has an implied end result, even if indirect (for instance, making the sponsor look good) – so there is always some beneficial outcome, and there must always be some way to measure it.

the vision thing

On the first page of his book *The Storm*, Vince Cable prefaces his analysis of the world economic crisis (2008 – and still ongoing as at 2016) with this comment: "individual and collective stupidity, greed and complacency act as powerful countervailing forces to what seems like unstoppable progress". There are parallels between country and global changes in financial markets, and divisional and global changes within an organisation. Missing from Cable's book, and the world, is a clear vision statement of where we want to be, coupled with a clearly-defined range of acceptable outcomes to achieve that vision. Without these, any major change programme is inefficient at best, and ineffective, unsustainable, and seriously damaging at worst. The challenge of creating these for a country let alone globally is immense, and with timescales far longer than the life of any democratic administration. In a large organisation it is hardly less challenging. Yet it must be done.

Vision is what it says – a single, simple statement describing the desired high-level outcome from a change, and typically most useful to senior or distant stakeholders who have no interest or time for any detail. The project team then translates the Vision into a set of outcomes, measurable benefits and impacts. This validates the Vision (and who among us has inherited an impractical or flawed Vision?), and starts to create the essential sense of belonging that turns a disparate set of people into a coherent team. If the Vision needs refinement, this is a job for the Sponsor, with advice or at least input from the project team.

Vision and Mission statements only say something meaningful if a negation of the statement still makes sense. "To serve our customers well" is a meaningless mission because "To serve our customers badly" is not an option for any sensible organisation. "To put our customers first" is slightly meaningful in that there are other things we can possibly put first such as market share or profit. No-one could accuse Ryanair of putting their customers first, their focus was clearly on market share and profit – until 2014 when they had a change of heart, which may have been driven by losses to competition or may simply have been their next stage in a grand strategy.

So my advice to those involved in writing Visions and Missions is to drop, or at least summarise, all the statements of the obvious, and focus on the discretionary differentiators. This is hard, of course, because it may not be attractive to include things like "maximise profit for shareholders" or "minimum contribution towards environmental degradation", and also because most competitive organisations are after the same things. One approach is to talk about *how* we achieve the obvious outcomes, which is where it is easier to differentiate: "best practice customer service using UK-based call centres" is a popular one (in the UK), as is "provide all staff with a career path through a combination of on-the-job and structured learning".

success criteria

Change is never free – it costs money, and time (which is more money) – so it's vital to have a clear & shared understanding of the criteria for success. Ultimately this is usually money in for-profit organisations, though sometimes indirectly so, such as reducing time-to-market, fewer disruptions, improved efficiency, or better publicity. In not-for-profit or the public sector, the ultimate aim is usually improved delivery of whatever service is provided, again with many indirect ways of getting there. The hospice charity with a chain of shops may change the stock control process so the shops make more money, whereas the ultimate aim is to use that money to deliver better hospice services to more people with cancer.

A bit of cost or time overrun is not necessarily a failure! I know that sounds like a heresy, when 'on time and to budget' is the popular mantra. But consider this: not delivering the benefits is definitely a failure. So it is not the cost & time that are most important, it is the benefits in relation to the cost & time.

That said, cost is the next most visible thing after time. It is best to define cost in the broadest sense ... in order to do this thing, what will we not have that we had before, at least in the short term until after the benefits have delivered? Money is the obvious thing, and certainly in business everything eventually translates back to money. It could be lives – what about the medical organisation funded by charity that works in war or disaster zones, do they assess how much extra loss of life is acceptable? Also look at the opportunity cost – if we do this what else will we not be able to do, and what are the consequences of that.

flexibility

There is rarely a single 'right' outcome nor a 100% certainty of achieving it. The real world is littered with random events and unknown factors which may affect our plans, usually at the worst possible moment. Of course the strategy seeks to anticipate as much as possible, however there still needs to be some flexibility.

We talk about internal flexibility later, but one potential area of flexibility is in the outcomes i.e. the benefits delivered. It is worth exploring whether there are 'good, better, best' options in the delivery of numbers, a time-box of acceptable dates, or a low-consequence switch between short, medium or long-term deliverables.

I generally advocate that dates are the last thing to shift. This is because they are the most easily visible and commonly understood feature of the outcome, and to shift them will decrease trust and may have unexpected knock-on effects. Dates are understood and relied upon, perhaps to a surprising extent, by people who know nothing else about the change.

The important point is that it is a lot less risky to think these things through up front. If we are doing the analysis after the disrupting factor has occurred, there is a danger of tactical or knee-jerk reactions that weaken the benefit. Furthermore, this early exploration acts as one more sanity check on the robustness of the outcome benefit. If indeed there is no room for flexibility at all, this tells us that we are probably on a high risk path – whether it is unacceptably high risk is of course dependent on the circumstances.

A useful tool for deciding on the priorities of a set of outcomes, or deliverables, is the MoSCoW rules. We simply assign things under one of 4 categories:

Must - non-negotiable, it must be delivered
Should - it must be delivered unless negotiated otherwise
Could - it could be delivered if it can be fitted in
Would - it would be delivered if there was more
    time/money/resources available

The discussion that justifies each assignment can be quite instructive and revealing.

minimum necessary change

In 1955 Isaac Asimov, the celebrated science fiction author, introduced the concept of Minimum Necessary Change (MNC) in his book *The End Of Eternity*. The context of his story is a little grander than ours here; it describes people who lived outside normal Time and who made alterations to events in order to make a safer future for mankind. Given it was written in the 50s, Asimov made some clever predictions about computing power and digital storage, and some prescient observations about the dangers of nuclear technology and the impracticality of space travel. The interesting point for us is that the Eternals, as they were called, could adjust future realities to huge effect with a tiny alteration in the past. One example was in the need to change the direction of a society with the choice of two actions between moving a container from one shelf to another or arranging a spaceship crash that killed many people. It's not hard to see the MNC there. Whilst this was fiction, and the changes were on an epic scale over immense timescales, the principle of the MNC for a desired outcome is very useful. It is echoed in a number of other theories and methods.

Occam's Razor is the principle that in explaining something, no more assumptions should be made than are necessary. Putting this another way, with a choice of explanations, or solutions or actions, the one with fewest assumptions is preferable. The same philosophy applies to selecting the minimum change for an outcome, and it comes down to reducing risk and uncertainty.

Alan Fowler and Dennis Lock in *Accelerating Business and IT Change: Transforming Project Delivery* define MNC as a term to describe the path of least change effort, cost and time to reach the outcome (not to be confused with critical path). This is something that underlies the effectiveness of Toyota's lean engineering of the 1970s and the step-change in the effectiveness of shipbuilding by the Koreans in the 1980s.

A simple example of this is where the customer approaches the supplier and says "we need to analyse our data in a more sophisticated way, so please deliver a new database, convert the data into it and train us how to use it". The commercially astute external supplier will ask the size of the available budget and whether it is signed off, before commencing a plan that ensures the whole budget gets spent with them. The agnostic change manager who is sitting between them starts by asking "what is the required outcome of the data analysis?", and discovers that the current database with a small configuration change will deliver 95% of what is required. This becomes the MNC. Now there may be all sorts of commercial, political and strategic reasons for still moving to a new database, but the MNC should be considered as a top candidate because we get most of the benefits in a much shorter timescale at hugely reduced risk and cost – what's not to like?!

Prepare to measure

We talk more about measurement, especially the timing of it, in Chapter 6. Here I want to make the general case for measurement being up there as one of the top activities for successful change, and then to focus on when measurement is not easy.

Ask ourselves three questions:

- if we do not measure the outcomes and benefits, how do we know that we have finished, and to what extent have we succeeded?
- if we do not agree up front how and when outcomes and benefits will be measured, how do we know that everyone has the same expectations?
- if we do not measure before the change, how can we put the measurements afterwards into perspective?

Whilst one would imagine and hope that the necessity for measurement is self-evident from this, I am going to labour the point a little further.

be selective and fair

You might (or you might not) be surprised to hear that in my experience of participating in change, often the benefits were seen to be self-evident and measurement was not even considered. I have been guilty of this myself in the past. Yet consider this; the change has a cost, and the budget for this expenditure will have been justified against the benefits it will deliver. Therefore someone, somewhere has (or should have) put a monetary value on the expected benefits. This implies some kind of measurement of current status, and identification of factors to measure later, although it may have been done by the finance department or senior management rather than the change team. If that is the case, the analysis or expectations may be unrealistic. To avoid this risk the change team must be at least involved, if not leading, the identification and process of measurement.

Looking at a different angle, measurement 'after' does not mean only at the completion of the whole change. Change programmes may come under pressure during their lives to release budget or resources for other competing programmes – they may even be mothballed or terminated. Change programmes may also be complex and with long timescales which makes it difficult to maintain a positive profile in people's minds. In these cases in particular it is very advantageous to deliver 'quick wins'. This means providing tangible benefits during the life of the programme, starting as early as possible, to make it 'real' from the boardroom to the floor. Now just because we call it a quick win does not mean that the delivery, training, publicity ... and *measurement* ... is quick. Quite the reverse. We may need to put in a disproportionate amount of time in supporting the quick win delivery, to ensure that detractors, sceptics and competing programmes cannot accuse us of delivering more disruption than benefit.

The way to avoid that accusation is in efficient and effective measurement before and after every benefit delivery.

It is worth taking great care about what we decide to measure, and when. Blastland and Dilnot in *The Tiger That Isn't* explain very clearly about accounting for natural cycles in our measurement targets, about choosing measures that are properly representative, about avoiding erroneous comparisons, and about avoiding the gaming of results. I recommend it highly.

One more general point is worth making where a change programme is deliberately delivering a local disbenefit. For instance, closing a department or a company or reducing a workforce due to poor company performance. Even here we can and must find things we can measure to demonstrate the effectiveness of the change programme.

where is the benefit?

The benefit arising from a change can be many things other than the obvious one of sustainable profit, or increased effectiveness in a non-profit organisation.

The proposition may be complex and the benefit may not be equally applicable to everyone involved (especially when replacing and reducing staff). Nevertheless, the consequences of failing to clearly explain the benefit will be rumours, wrong expectations, poor decision-making, lack of commitment, inefficiency, delays ... both inside and outside the organisation.

Measuring outputs rather than inputs was the mantra of the late 20th century. In other words it is not enough, or sometimes not even necessary, to 'work hard'. Measuring the effort put in or the cost of that effort (resources, services, equipment) alone is not meaningful. Despite that obvious observation there is still, at the time of writing, an element of 'presenteeism' where salaried people are valued (or value themselves) by the long hours they work and by working despite being ill. It may be that they are highly productive for all those hours, and this is what fulfils them, in which case the organisation is indeed getting value for money. The more common scenarios are that either the employee is having difficulty keeping up, or that after a period as a bright flame they burn out through exhaustion – neither of which is good for them or the organisation. The same mantra applies to individuals and to projects. Measure the outputs, by all means related to the inputs, and while we are at it measure the well-being of the people at the same time.

One other distinction is worth making in looking for benefit; measure the impact of the outcome, not just the raw outcome and certainly not other factors. Take an example of making a fire to warm the room. If we make it using newly cut logs we will get plenty of noise, as it spits, and some light but little heat. If we use kindling and coal in a large open fireplace there will be plenty of heat but it goes up the chimney rather than into the room. A kindling and coal fire in an enclosed fireplace with draught control will deliver a lot of heat to the room. So if heat in the room is what we want, don't measure associated factors like noise and light, and don't just measure the heat … measure where it goes.

illustration: seeing is believing

British Airways were moving to a new Terminal building, one that was much larger than previous buildings and incorporating the latest technology for managing passengers and their bags. A large change programme was in place, which included a team focused on changing the business processes used to manage passengers from Check-in to the Boarding Gate. This work ran in parallel with the building work, so everyone was working from architects' drawings. The team found it difficult to relate to the benefit of their work, compared to Flight Management and Baggage Handling changes that had obvious physical challenges.

"Our processes are just people sitting around, reading displays and walking." So the programme manager arranged for the team to have a tour of the half-finished building.

They donned hard hats and steel-toed boots and, stepping carefully over and around equipment, tools and cables, they walked the routes that the passengers would take. This physical experience brought home to them the scale of the building and increased distances for passengers, which would especially affect the young and the elderly. Then they understood the critical benefit of well-positioned signage and displays to reduce the risk of people getting lost or disoriented, and how both flight management and baggage handling timings would be reliant on their accurate time estimates for passenger transits across the building.

It is not the cost & time alone that are important, it is the benefits in relation to the cost & time, as we established in a previous segment.

The benefit must be defined in terms of measurable and practical deliverables, and must be a combination of short, medium and long-term deliverables. If the short term is going to be nothing but pain, then say so. (If the long term is nothing but pain, then our strategy may be somewhat flawed.)

The benefit must be expressed in high-level framework terms to which all participants can relate equally, and then again in more specific terms to each group in a way that is relevant to their participation. Staff, partners and suppliers, for instance, each need different information, encouragement and calls to action, all within the consistent benefit framework. It is helpful to all concerned to express this benefit not just in terms of the organisation concerned, but also in the broader context of the market and environment within which the organisation operates.

fuzzy benefits

Measurement can be a challenge when the benefits are not easily quantifiable. There *is* always a measure, we just have to think around it, think laterally. Doing so may make us re-think the priorities.

Tom Gilb has been practicing, teaching and preaching about focusing on benefits and their measurement for decades. In 2013 he gave a TEDx talk on *Quantifying the Unquantifiable* in which he demonstrates the approach to measuring love:

> Love has many components, a central one being ...
>> Trust which is established in many ways, a central one being ...
>>> Truthfulness which in principle, at least, can be measured as ...
>>>> Lies per month, in various grades

so in that way, to some extent, even a part of Love can be quantified.

The best approach, as above, to defining large fuzzy outcome benefits is to break things down (decompose) into components, parts or pieces in order to grapple with quantifying them. This is sometimes called Cartesian analysis. Then build up the combination of measures with weightings and priorities as appropriate to the needs. This also ensures common understanding and expectation.

As well as fuzziness in the outcomes we can easily have fuzziness in the factors affecting the delivery of the change. If we cannot accurately measure the factor then measure its fuzziness and multiply that by its impact on the delivery. This is in the same realm as risk management, where we assess the size of the risk by multiplying the likelihood of it happening by the impact if it happens.

Working back … and forward

In this section we are assuming that there is an agreed, aspirational set of required outcomes. I have a lot more to say about ways to validate and refine the outcomes, and the bear-traps on the way, in Chapters 4 and 5; for now we'll look at how we validate (or indeed invalidate) through planning the journey from here to there.

As we have discussed in the previous sections, without a set of targets we are at the mercy of every puff of wind and every stakeholder whim. If we don't work back from the targets in terms of establishing what needs to be done, then there can be no predictability – and predictability generates trust – and trust removes barriers.

It is also true to assert that we have to work forward in our planning. It is perfectly acceptable to do the working forward and working back with different teams at the same time. Inevitably they will not meet perfectly in the middle. The manner and the extent to which they miss each other will be instructive. One or both will need adjustments until the forward and the back views are coherent and perfectly joined up.

Sometimes we really do have to find out what exactly is required as we do the work; this is practical as long as everyone understands the status. Acknowledge when our starting point is based upon guesstimates, and plan for reviews and re-working accordingly, accepting that there may be radical alterations.

asking questions

In the **Forward in the fog** section earlier we discussed critical thinking and also good and bad questions. I encourage you to question everything, yet in a sensitive and constructive manner of course. Ask ourselves 'do I understand this' and then 'do I believe this'. In many cases we can answer our own questions through our own knowledge and experience, and through documents, presentations and web content available to us.

In this chapter's fiction, were the staff good at asking questions? No, far from it. They made conscious and unconscious assumptions and jumped at the first thing in front of their noses. It took the catalyst of the experienced change manager for them to see the benefits of thinking around the immediate problem and asking some searching questions.

When asking questions of our colleagues there is an amplifier effect. Questions properly put will open up understanding and expose gaps and assumptions. If they are badly put, they cause defensiveness and alienation; 5 bad minutes can require 2 days to restore confidence and trust.

So ensure the recipient is open to the question, by understanding how they like to work and what pressures they might be under. Ask it in a non-threatening manner, being careful about our body language and our tone of voice as well as the wording. A useful phrase to soften the start is "It would be helpful if [you could explain ...] [I could understand ...] [we could validate ...]".

Having asked a good question, do not let go until the answers make sense and are verifiable, until we can both understand and believe them. Again this has to be done sensitively without irritating or alienating people, so don't act like a terrier (especially no growling). On the other hand be sure they realise that you won't let the question drift, and do your best to enlist their support in getting to the bottom of the proper answer.

Don't ask closed questions because we'll always get one answer. "Are you cost sensitive?" will always generate "yes!" Instead ask comparative, open questions to establish relative priorities, e.g. "can you rank your sensitivity against cost, time, quality, functionality?"

When we ask, or indeed invite, good questions in a constructive manner, we engage the other person and increase their sense of participation and belonging. This is an argument for asking easy questions where we are pretty sure of the answer already. We might do this simply as a way of creating and improving relationships, or we might be wanting to establish some trust and confidence before moving on to some more difficult questions.

---

illustration: don't ignore crucial questions

Within a few days of joining a growing change team I was asking the right questions ... about company structure, operational responsibilities and a business strategy to match the financial business case spreadsheet. Yet those questions got ignored or lost in the morass of detail and the management exhortation to get going ... and it was not my role to resolve them, nor was it possible on my own. Many of those questions were still extant months later when the implementation programme was rolling, causing confusion among new joiners and hampering strategic decisions, and I wished I had pursued it. The lack of agreed structures and strategies allowed for a lot of flexing and political manoeuvring, and possibly this was a deliberate strategy in itself, for the senior management to keep options open. In my view the typical change team has enough uncertainty to nail down within the programme, without having to live with such high-level uncertainties sitting above them.

---

timing and timescales

It is rare to not have some date target or constraint for the change. Sometimes this is soft, as in "if we get it done before the year-end it will have a greater impact". Sometimes this is hard, as in "we have to complete this in time for the change in the law on April 6th".

Of course all Changes must be completed within the allotted time, even if that was a wild guess or simply a statement of desire by senior management that then needs significant correction. The strategy of 'bad news early' is never more important than here; timing is about delivering messages to stakeholders at the earliest possible moment when the message will be heard and understood. Choose your moment for receptiveness.

Timescale is a different issue; many of the world's problems, from population to environment to economy, require a change strategy that is far longer than the term of the people elected to deal with it - their temptation is then to apply tactics until they can exit. Beware of this within the organisation, it is human nature. For a long-term change, we need to break it into shorter-term deliverables & benefits, and we need to find a way for the overall change strategy to survive management generations.

assumptions and dependencies

It is very rare for the various components of a change to be unconnected with each other and unaffected by external statuses or events. Most commonly these components are actioned in a context, in a sea of connections with varying degrees of impact on, or threat to, the change.

The distinction between assumptions, dependencies and risks can easily be confused, as they can be seen to overlap. There is no point at all in recording something in more than one of these categories – that just leads to duplication.

Every respectable programme or project maintains a series of lists or logs, where status information is captured and assessed. Does a dependency go in the Risk Log? No, because a risk is something that *might* happen, whereas a dependency is something that *will* happen or *is* happening. Does a dependency go on the Assumptions Log, then? We could do that, although my preference is to maintain a separate Dependency Log for clarity. Assumptions in my mind are passive things (e.g. no regulatory change in the next 6 months), whereas dependencies are active (staff training is required before process delivery). Should a dependency that is in trouble go on the Issue Log? We could do that, however I prefer to manage statuses in the Dependency Log.

Assumptions are often not even acknowledged, let alone critically examined. After all, they are assumptions, right? Everyone knows about them and there is no risk there, oh no. Yet in our assumptions could lurk the seeds of our undoing. Assumptions must be flushed out, reviewed, and removed where at all possible. And at a micro level, check that spreadsheet – how reliable and accurate is that bottom row of figures, really?

---

digression: government fiscal assumptions

When the UK Government provides projections showing the Budget Deficit decreasing nicely over the next 5 years, do they list the underlying assumptions they have made in a form accessible to the public? They do not, and if you search online you will at best find scattered individual assumptions rather than a comprehensive and impact-ordered list. Furthermore many 'assumptions' are in fact policy decisions or aspirations as in "spending will be reduced by x%".

Could it be that they think we would not understand? I'm sure it is complex, but it would still be better if the media could have a crack at explaining it. I suspect instead that the concern is whether we will see that the emperor has no clothes, that the assumptions are selected and massaged to ensure a positive picture. After all, what government would predict that we are heading for disaster in four years' time?

Usually there are a variety of dependencies in logistics, resources, even money both within the project and also between the project and other activities inside and outside the organisation. Also most commonly not all dependencies are understood or even visible. A crucial part of the initial planning, working backwards and forwards, is to dig out the dependencies and bring them blinking into the daylight. They may radically affect the overall plan, possibly even alter the strategy or the practically achievable outcomes.

The assembled list of dependencies will doubtless be expanded as more detailed planning and design is carried out, and the list must be monitored and updated continuously throughout the life-cycle of the change.

If we have a large number of interconnected dependencies with unclear priority or sequence, then something has to be done. Indeed it is always good to find ways to minimise and simplify dependencies, to reduce the likelihood of problems. The best approach starts, as is so often the case, by asking good questions and doing some critical and inventive thinking. Sometimes dependencies are there out of habit or false assumptions. Sometimes they can be unhooked by quite small adjustments. It may even be acceptable to increase the time or cost of a change if doing so makes it significantly simpler and more predictable (although this can take some arguing).

The best way to simplify and minimise a functional dependency is to define the simplest common interface between the two or more components. This is a well-established technique when building computer systems, and can equally be applied to business processes and service models. The components can then be built and tested independently, and in extremis one can be delivered whilst another is manually operated, as long as the interface is maintained. Naturally the interface definition must be owned and managed at the highest level in the change project, because any alterations will have significant consequences for multiple teams.

strive for simple

Look for the simplest solutions, by working up from the dirty detail, and by working back from the simple vision.

When we have a big meaty problem, describe the simple straight-line solution even though it is unacceptable, untenable and unworkable ... and then start working back with compromises and adjustments until it becomes workable. This is a way to get as close as possible to the ideal solution. For example, the unacceptable straight-line solution to the cost of caring for the aged-unwell population is to force their children to live nearby and look after them, just like the good old days when families and communities stayed together and supported themselves.

There are many sailing metaphors that could be employed. I have limited myself to just one. It is called 'Course to Steer'. When a sailing boat is leaving point A and wishes to arrive at point B, there are many factors to consider.

The navigator gets out the chart(s) containing points A and B, and starts by drawing a straight line between them. That's the obvious route, and apparently the most efficient.

Although sailing is a highly unpredictable business due to the weather and other boats, the factors such as tides, daylight and the physical hazards are very well defined and tabulated and mapped. If only a business change could be plotted on a chart containing all known hazards, and those hazards don't move, then how much easier life would be?

The first point is that the straightest line may hold dangers. Clearly specific dangers such as land and rocks and shallows must be avoided, and potential dangers such as shipping lanes are to be avoided, or traversed according to regulations. So the navigator plots a course consisting of numerous 'legs' or straight-line sections, that travel through safe water. The next challenge is to steer (helm) the boat along each of these lines without unsafe deviation. The factors here are the weather, the tide, the drift of the boat, the accuracy/dependability of the instruments, and the quality of the helming. Because on the water there is no direct evidence at any one time as to where we are. Well, there is if we have a GPS chart plotter and it is working (the equivalent of satnav in cars). The consequences of not knowing where we are, or worse still not being where we believe we are, can easily be expensive, and even life-threatening. Also true in a project – if not life-threatening, the stress can be injurious to health.

We need to think through the known and potential hazards and plot the project's course around them. The requirement for the best route, whether sailing or in a change project, is to plot a course that has well understood and manageable risks with early warning of deviations and unexpected events.

Governance & structure

We need to glance forward here, to the How Change Is Managed section at the start of Chapter 5, and the simple diagram that shows governance sitting on top of the change structure. That diagram does simplify real life, because of course governance and structure are needed throughout all the areas and activities, both in the change effort and in the business-as-usual work.

As with all things, these management tools need to be as simple as possible while being fit-for-purpose. It is all too easy to overdo it, through lack of trust or anxiety or the need for control, and in so doing strangle the effectiveness of individuals and teams.

The approach to and success of change is affected by many attributes of the organisation; one of the most important is the management structure and style. The models of command & control, benevolent dictator, consensus led and empower & delegate all have very different consequences for the planning and execution of the change.

Governance may be thought of as the boring stuff, yet it must be done well, or at the first hiccup the change programme will all fall apart. Here is what I say to clients when setting this up: "Whatever you do, don't humour me – I am only interested in achieving positive agreement. If you don't understand something, question me ferociously. If you disagree with something, argue back with alternatives. If you think I'm duplicating or re-inventing, point me towards what's been done before."

governance principles

The main practical benefits of a governance structure are:

- keep change programmes honest via active reviews
- provide a suitable authority for decision-making above the change programme
- protect and champion the change in the context of the whole organisation

The frequency and depth of reviews, the process for escalating decisions, and the methods of championing are all things that vary according to the size and nature of both the change and the organisation.

alignment with BAU

Again I suggest that we start with the end in mind. In this case I am talking about the governance or management structure. The transition of the change into the normal business operation is considerably eased if thought is given at the outset to the governance handover as well.

Clearly the operational business have a governance structure, often more commonly called a management structure in this context. It is likely to have been set up by, or in collaboration with, the HR department; there will have been some 'organisational development' at some point to establish the current layers, groupings and reporting lines and processes to ensure the business runs smoothly.

HR probably has a strong interest in the handover of our change, and they should be involved right at the beginning of the project. Not only to assist in designing a fit-for-purpose change governance structure that can deliver smoothly into the operational one, but also for their advice and involvement in any and all people issues within the change itself before it delivers.

checks, balances & decisions

An essential part of the governance is an independent assurance role – not to find fault or play politics, but to act as an advisor, challenger and reviewer with an outside viewpoint. Someone without blinkers or vested interest. This may be a part-time role or it may need multiple people, depending on the size of the change. Whoever is doing this must have no other role or involvement in the change; there must be no conflict of interest, no loyalty other than to the success of the change.

For effective decision-making there must be clear structures, in terms of meetings, reporting, responsibilities and matching authority, escalation paths – the regular flows and the ad-hoc ones. There must be single points of responsibility, and no single points of failure. All of this must be documented as part of the governance structure.

Poor or untimely decision-making can easily maim or kill a perfectly good change project, and it is possible for a small hesitation to generate an avalanche of indecision and uncertainty. Be clear on how decisions are made and by whom, and acknowledge that there are hard decisions, and agree that decisions have to be made to keep moving forward, and accept that we may make some sub-optimal decisions.

---

illustration: independent assurance balance

Royal Mail is essentially a service organisation, to consumers and business. When embarking upon a programme to delivery some significant changes to their operation, they were only too aware of under-achievements in the past due to vested interests and inexperience watering down the change delivery. This time they decided to have someone providing independent assurance to the programme board which was at the top of the governance tree for this change. First they tried someone from the operational team but they were too close, they got involved in far too much detail. Then they tried a change expert from outside the organisation but they were too far, they didn't understand the business and its language and history. Then they tried someone from a different division of the organisation, one unaffected by these changes, and they were just right because they understood the challenges, asked good questions and gave honest opinions.

---

documents

We need pragmatic, fit-for-purpose documentation standards (I have seen everything from no identity whatsoever to a full government-style front page for a half-page memo). Ideally a standard goes across the whole organisation, and at least across the whole change activity. Without this, time is often wasted and wrong information can be acted upon.

Every document must have author, date and file location as an absolute minimum, with version numbers and change/review history for standing or reference documents. Every page must have the document title and page number. One standing document that is always helpful yet rarely provided is a Glossary of Terms.

There must be a shared electronic repository for documents accessible by everyone, plus shared calendar. This should only have access control levels if it is absolutely necessary.

Self-describing file structures are very helpful, and it is best to keep it very simple. I am not always good at practicing what I preach. Looking back at some Index & Navigation files from a programme 5 years ago I found myself thinking "wow, this is probably clever, but I can't understand it now". Clearly it wasn't simple enough.

I realise this whole Governance section may look bureaucratic and cumbersome – that is absolutely *not* what I'm about – pragmatism is a wonderful thing. It is the principles that are essential, and the simpler the implementation the better.

Speak truth to power

In *Tony Benn – A Political Life* by David Powell, the long-standing British MP observed "it isn't so much that power corrupts, as the cosy feeling that you are part of a little club running the country".

This can happen in organisations too. The Sponsor, the Stakeholders, and the Board don't always know everything, and don't always know what is best in a particular situation. They have been known to issue edicts without knowing or thinking through the practicalities and the consequences. These are examples of 'statements of desire' because they define a future status, often with time and cost constraints, with no reference to the practicality of getting there or the measurable benefits to be realised.

The difficulty comes in challenging their assumptions, goals or aspirations, without appearing to challenge their authority or capability. They are, after all, accountable people in a position of power.

This chapter's fiction shows a reluctance to even engage with the external 'power' – the Regulatory Inspector. The company was about to enter a downward spiral of over-promising, under-delivery and loss of trust. Instead through treating the 'power' with respect but not unquestioning awe they constructively negotiated to work on reliable promises and demonstrated they are in control of the situation.

This constructive challenging is not only needed at the outset of the change, although that is where it has the biggest benefit. There may well be a need for it at any or all stages of the change cycle, although it is not a full-time job. This role may be filled by the change manager, as long as their only incentive is the success of the change. Alternatively it can be covered by the assurance role discussed in the Governance section earlier, or there can be an external 'change strategist' who does this as part of an expert guidance role. The choice of approach depends on the size and complexity of the change, the extent to which management is open to challenge, and perhaps even the history of changes in the organisation.

challenge for clarity

We must share and understand a simple definition of what we are doing and why – something any of us can explain to anyone – this serves as a baseline, an outer envelope (choose your metaphor) against which we checkpoint the detail and complexities – it also strengthens our sense of identity and purpose.

Of course, we say to them, you people in power know all this. It is just that other people involved in the change will benefit from having it spelled out (and I can help you do that).

The 'challenger' must be impartial, with no emotional or political baggage to cloud their judgement. They can be agnostic on the quality of the commercial rationale for the change, it is not for them to double-guess the investors' or board's approach. However they may (or indeed should) say something if it seems to them that the strategy is driving towards a cliff. What they do need is a thorough understanding of the rationale, in order to manage the communication, structuring and prioritisation of the change.

The challenger must question, drill down and play devil's advocate to tease out and sanity check the vision, the expectations, the deliverables, dependencies and risks. It is better that they are not a subject matter expert in the business, because they must ask the 'dumb' questions and in some cases they must 'say the unsayable'.

For all these reasons it is very important to choose our challenger and his/her reporting line very carefully. It can be someone from inside the organisation, although there are hidden dangers: they may be 'too close to the wood and only see the trees', they may have difficulty with the new relationships and reporting, they may be worried about their next performance review. It could be a suitably experienced investor, or other external stakeholder, as long as their agenda is perfectly aligned. Or an increasingly successful model is to use a professional interim, someone from outside the organisation who has done this before and specialises in this type of work.

As to the reporting line, there may be multiple lines if that helps to tie the whole picture together, and they should be as senior as possible. One reporting line must go to the senior executive or other stakeholder who is the overall champion for the change, and to whom the challenger can turn if they run out of fire power.

ask yet more questions

Always assume nothing is obvious. Be careful to check common understanding, check common assumptions, check common expectations. We have to dress it up as our need rather than the senior management's to avoid apparently insulting them. Depending on the individual we may be able to say "it is hardly practical for you to be across all the details of this, so let me just check off a few things with you to be absolutely sure we deliver what you expect".

It is not unknown to be told that something is not relevant or affected because the management do not want it to be so; that is not a good enough reason to exclude it. Always test the edges of the envelope. Keep working out and up and down until we demonstrably reach a point that is very definitely out of scope or relevance. If we are familiar with at least one layer outside our remit we can better understand the context of the change and the perspective of everyone outside the change; this helps enormously with communication.

choose our moment

Most people in a position of power do not welcome being challenged in a public forum or a large meeting, no matter how sensitively phrased. Equally if we get the brush-off it is difficult to pursue in that situation.

It is far better to explore the point in a one-to-one or small meeting, and it is better if the setting is informal. We are not seeking to disempower the boss, and so we need the solution or action to come from them eventually, or at least appear to come from them.

Criticising individuals or situations inevitably leads to defensiveness and a closing of minds. The best way to focus attention on the issue is to describe the disbenefits if nothing is done to improve matters. Then it becomes a question of "what can we do to avoid ...". Note the deliberate use of 'we' there to include the listener(s) in the action. By the end of the discussion it becomes their action, even their initiative, and all is well.

suicide avoidance

Changes are sometimes created to further someone's personal agenda, to illustrate their power, or as a knee-jerk reaction to a problem. These are often the most ill-conceived initiatives. The clear danger is that all involved with the change become tarred with the same brush when it goes wrong or creates upheaval.

Very occasionally there may be the feeling that you are all driving towards a cliff, and you are the only one that can see it. If the steering and braking discussed earlier in this section don't work, then you should find a way to bail out. Doing that, or even announcing it, might just be the final wake-up call to management before it is too late. Of course this is immensely difficult to do, and I never advocate threatening to walk away from a problem unless that is absolutely the very last tool in the box to avoid a disaster.

Takeaways

- avoid the impulse to 'just get started'
- use critical thinking and ask good questions
- make no assumptions and be constructively challenging at the right times
- analyse and assess on the broadest possible basis, look for inclusion and prove exclusion
- look for the minimum necessary change to achieve the required outcomes
- minimise dependencies, always look for simplicity
- plan by working backwards from the required outcomes, and working forward from now
- if we cannot measure it, we cannot deliver it
- predictability generates trust, and trust removes barriers
- the right governance structure keeps everyone honest
- those in power will listen to truth when delivered in the right way at the right time

4 Strategies and Tactics

The slam of the meeting room door emphasised the Chief Operating Officer's shouted question "How the HELL did we get into this situation?" Olaf, the Project Manager looked across at Carla, the Communications Lead and Mohammed, the Quality Manager, trying to judge who might answer. Not that the COO really wanted an answer, she should know the background by now; what she really wanted, and should have asked, is "how the hell are we going to recover this situation?" However, when your COO is angry it is best not to overtly contradict. Better to briefly handle the question and quickly move onto more positive ground. All of this flashed through Olaf's mind as he watched the body language of Carla and Mohammed while the shouted question hung in the air.

"There are a number of complex factors" Olaf volunteered into the uncomfortable silence, "but in summary I think we have been too focused on the detail and no-one has been actively managing the bigger picture". Olaf was conscious he could be digging a hole that became his own grave, and Carla and Mohammed were looking on with interest. "What I mean" he continued "is that we've all been working hard within our own responsibilities, each of us making lots of assumptions about what the others are doing."

The COO glared at him and spat out "so it's Carla's fault then is it for not communicating?" "No, it's not as simple as that" replied Olaf quickly "and I'm not trying to assign blame; I just think we are lacking overall co-ordination of the work we are doing and the effect it will have across the company and its suppliers."

"Look, it's simple" said the COO a little more calmly, but still grimly, leaning on the table and clearly not yet ready to sit down "this is an operational change within one division to replace a billing system. It's just mechanics, and it's up and running now on time and in budget. The clients don't need to know. But the Finance Director just told me that due to us the company is not receiving payments from our clients and is heading towards a cashflow problem." More shifting in chairs before Mohammed spoke up "I agree with Olaf; the quality of the individual pieces of work has been fine, but changes in bill timing, categorisation codes and the new corporate CRM system have had unexpected effects on the clients." "What I'm hearing" added Carla "is that clients don't understand the new invoices and are therefore unwilling to pay against them." Mohammed jumped back in, keen to rationalise his position "The original assumption was that the clients would see no difference in the billing. However we've had a number of small changes through the project, each individually justified and correctly signed off, and now we are seeing the cumulative effect."

Olaf knew that the COO was only interested in 'now and next week' and had little patience with long-term planning. With her as project sponsor there was always going to be a tussle between tactics and strategy. Yet now that tactics had led them into a problem, perhaps he could get away with some strategising to address the question the COO should have asked. "I suggest our strategy now is three-fold: we keep the system we have built, making only a minimum of configuration changes and no more customisation; we document our design approach, inter-dependencies and corporate benefits achieved, for discussion and negotiation with affected divisions especially the CRM people; and we provide a script for the account directors to explain the changes and associated benefits in individual client meetings."

Finally the COO sat down, and thought for a moment. "Ok, I want all that done by the end of this week so I can get the FD off my back". Olaf smiled at Carla and Mohammed, thinking here we are again, back to the tactics. The Lesson Learned about needing a Change Manager at the outset, to handle the wider implications and expectations, would have to wait until the heat was off.

Any change that is even a modest step for an organisation has many factors, including external dependencies, stakeholders, resourcing, measurable benefits, acceptable outcomes, timing, brand impact, customer satisfaction and of course cost.

A strategy for change must take a panoptic view of the organisation and the context in which it operates and plans to change. Above all, it must think ahead and pre-handle as many scenarios as possible, to protect the required outcome whilst adjusting the route to get there. This means not only looking across the whole change, but also above, below and alongside as well, taking the big picture into account and including all the external factors and influences.

Strategy is something we have before we start, and we only alter it very slowly and carefully, and we maintain it until after the change is completed. We sign up for an achievable vision, bringing all the factors together, balancing conflicts, pre-handling issues, creating and pursuing a high-level, long-term roadmap, and constantly looking for new threats and objections.

Tactics, on the other hand, are something that we develop during the work as circumstances arise, often within the details of the implementation. Of course we can plan ahead with tactics too, although by definition they are short-term, alterable and disposable.

The story above is one of a strategy that is too narrow, if it existed at all at the outset. Certainly it has not addressed anything outside the mechanical changes being made. The way out of the problem is largely tactical, although the project manager is doing his best to put it into a strategic framework or context. It is likely this organisation will repeat the mistake unless there is a strong commitment to both recording and using Lessons Learned, and thinking more broadly.

Confusion is natural

Strategy and Change are inextricably interwoven. Any change, no matter how modest, must have a strategy to protect it from internal and external pressures (see Chapter 6) and from blockers and distractions (see Chapter 7).

Richard Rumelt in *Good Strategy/Bad Strategy* identifies that a good strategy does more than urge us towards a goal or vision; it honestly acknowledges the challenges faced and provides an approach to overcoming them. He talks about a strategy kernel that contains a diagnosis, a guiding policy, and coherent action. Unfortunately good strategy is the exception, not the rule, in my experience and observation. More and more organisations espouse a bad strategy that skips over pesky details such as problems, and is no more than a statement of desire. As we discussed in earlier chapters, statements of desire are very common and rather dangerous, all the more so when wrapped up and presented as a strategy. Rumelt goes on to look at the differences between good and bad strategies with many examples from commercial and governmental organisations; his view is that the creeping spread of bad strategy, that takes on a life and logic of its own, a false edifice built on a mistaken foundation, affects us all – we must demand more from those who lead.

Differing incentives, understandings, expectations ... this is what makes working on strategy so interesting. It's like constructing or even designing a 3-dimensional jigsaw. This is often difficult when senior stakeholders are shouting in our ear "c'mon, let's get going, let's show some progress!"

It is helpful to visualise strategy as a continuous arc from 'here' to 'there', encompassing the whole picture and everything external that might affect it. Visualise tactics as short darts or bursts of activity that may be off from the ideal direction, even reversing it on rare occasions, to deal with specific situations or problems.

illustration: wind of change

An example of something requiring strategy is wind energy. There are problems and mixed results today including the challenge of energy storage. Yet looking ahead it seems very likely we will reach a time (if not already) when fossil fuels are scarce, very expensive or simply too destructive. So we need to evolve other technologies and sources now, even if in the short term they appear flawed and too costly. As long as there is no law of physics against them, we can and will figure them out with new science. This science takes time, and so we need to be working on it long before the 'crunch' point. The difficulty here is that the timescales are longer than a typical politician's tenure, and the temptation in government can be towards tactics that generate apparent benefits (for the populace or government) in years rather than decades or centuries. A successful strategy in this type of situation is one that delivers some benefits within the timescale of the instigators, whilst aiming for greater benefits to the generations to come.

change and BAU

It is possible to have a strategy that does not involve a change. A strategy to maintain the business-as-usual or status quo is quite normal, such as when faced with an outside threat to stability. This should come under the same gimlet scrutiny espoused by Rumelt.

More commonly an organisation is a rolling combination of varying proportions of BAU and change activities. There is often poor distinction between the two, if people are not thinking clearly enough about the end result. This distinction is necessary, though, because BAU and Change have very different dynamics, different messages and incentives for the people involved. Part of the strategy, then, must recognise and include the BAU elements that are related to, intersect with, and are altered by the change.

It may be that the same people are working in both modes (at different times) through the period of the change. I generally consider this to be a bad idea, because unexpected events in BAU are always a higher priority than the project, and so the project loses control over its resources. Nevertheless, in small organisations this may be unavoidable. In which case it is vital that people understand which mindset they are in on any given day. The strategy may need to include extra management, and contingency plans for a resourcing crisis.

complicated or complex

Whilst most dictionaries define these two words as synonyms, there is a difference in the common usage when related to organisations and change projects. To my mind, 'complex' refers to an unavoidably large number of interconnecting factors and dependencies which is a feature of the modern world. Whereas 'complicated' refers to the difficulty of an individual understanding and managing the whole picture. So 'complex' is a fact of life to be dealt with, and 'complicated' is a state to be mitigated or avoided where possible. To put it another way, 'complex' is a factual description, whereas 'complicated' is a negative perception that inhibits performance.

Yves Morieux, of Boston Consulting Group (BCG), in a paper called *Smart Rules: Six Ways to Get People to Solve Problems Without You,* makes some very interesting points about complexity and complicatedness. BCG's research across 100 companies and over the last 50 years suggests that organisational complicatedness has risen by 35 times as a response to business complexity increasing by 6 times. Complicatedness is the square of complexity, it would seem, and this is due to the amount of procedures, vertical layers, interface structures, coordination bodies, and decision approvals needed – the complicatedness arises also from the need to keep decision-making and responsibilities at a human scale. As BCG say "In and of itself, this complexity is not a bad thing—it brings opportunities as well as challenges. The problem is the way companies attempt to respond to it." BCG's solution, in summary, is to empower and incentivise staff to cooperate and find solutions locally rather than escalating problems and decision-making.

My own observation is that this is fine, indeed I applaud it, yet it is only part of the approach needed to reduce the complicatedness. The strategy for an organisation, or just for a project, must include the selection of people who are good at handling a very broad responsibility, as part of reducing the hierarchical management layers towards the 'flat structure' espoused by many modern organisational experts. The strategy must also include communications (and more of this a little later) that acknowledge and handle the complexities, and yet sweep away the complicatedness.

trees and woods

I have been in situations where we have a large programme of work in a complex environment, and little things are going wrong. We use tactical actions to solve the problems that arise, and yet there are ever more problems. We are so focused on the trees, the detail in front of us each day, that we don't see the wood which is the larger context in which we are working.

When we do step back and look up we realise, to switch metaphors, that we are on a runaway train where no amount of small adjustments will resolve the larger problem. There is little point in fixing the coffee machine if the driver has fallen off the train. In such a situation we need to see it for what it is, and understand the cumulative effect, and instead of tinkering ... do something drastic. This is also good for morale, to acknowledge the overall problem as something that is shared and resolved together. The drastic action is usually something to regain the existing strategy. On occasion it may require a significant update to that strategy, which is an action never to be undertaken lightly.

Strategise to clear the mind

If the need for the change is obvious to all, the money is unconditionally available, and all stakeholders are unreservedly in favour, then we might think we do not need much of a strategy, we just need tactical management of a list of tasks and dates. To this I say "no, we always need a strategy" for two big reasons: first, if something sounds too good to be true, it probably is, and so there will be some problems and challenges hidden away; and second, factors alter even over a short time, so the completely favourable circumstances may not last.

In this chapter's opening story there is an apparently simple and uncontroversial change that almost brings the company to its knees, because there is no strategy. Due to the lack of a wider perspective, with no-one thinking about the bigger picture, the cumulative effect of multiple small and innocent changes has a dramatic outcome. The very well-defined and narrow remit of the change does not guarantee success.

The more common situation when first considering a change is that the desk is littered with uncertainties and unknowns, along with knowledge and suspicions of risks and issues that will arise later. It can become overwhelming to try and consider all factors at once.

Clarity is what is needed. Clarity of information, of thinking, of communication, and of action. This is the way we stay sane, and keep everyone with us.

getting started

My advice is to avoid diving into the detail. Instead, keep a clear head and write a strategy as a short, simple document. Avoid thinking with blinkers by asking ourselves, and all stakeholders, all the big questions:

- why do we need to do this
- what happens if we wait a year

- what could possibly go wrong
- who is dependent on this
- what other changes could impact this

Sometimes the question is not whether to make a certain change or not, but rather the best time, or least-worst time, to make it.

Devil's Advocacy is a much needed technique to force the consideration of alternatives, and the justification of choices. Ask ourselves and others really searching questions, say the unsayable, to see what it flushes out.

It is very hard to get something absolutely right the first time we do it, and we should consider these options:

1. take the time to deliberately do a dry-run, proof-of-concept, pilot, or beta, as a separate project up front
2. accept it will be 80% right and fit-for-purpose with improvements later
3. take a lot longer to get started, pulling in all the external experience we can get, to make the one shot our best shot

The most successful option depends on the certainty of the required outcomes, the appetite for risk in the organisation, and the priorities and trade-off between the four generic factors (which are further explored in the next chapter):

- time
- cost
- function
- quality

Sometimes before we can consider these strategic choices, we need to investigate the capability of the organisation – the skills and experience of the workforce, and the vision and confidence of the management.

A note of warning if you are working as an interim manager: we have to understand what makes the organisation tick, what drives it and where does it want to be ... and that is not always what they tell us at the interview or when we arrive. Assume nothing, ask lots of constructive questions, and do not let go until you have credible answers.

One more plea: never make decisions based on or influenced by emotions, always decide on facts ... and have a good strategy and plan to understand and manage the emotions.

---

illustration: Private Equity strategy

The changes initiated in a Private Equity context are rarely of a minor or incremental nature. They are usually significant, structural, even disruptive. Yet at the same time there is value to be protected. Intellectual capital is an important, sometimes crucial part of that value - in other words, there are key people throughout the organisation (not just near the top) who need to be retained in a positive engagement.

Equally there are stakeholders and influencers within and outside the organisation who need to maintain a clear and common understanding of the main aspects of the change, without being troubled by the detail. Furthermore the change is often dependent upon, or affected by, factors outside the control of the organisation: the global economy is the obvious example; in some industries it might be the weather; in others, perhaps availability of raw materials.

---

do surveys help?

Strategy is about defining long-term objectives and the high-level roadmap to achieving them. In companies this is most often set by the senior management, from their own experience and aspirations. In voluntary organisations, associations, industry bodies and other groups, and even some political parties, it is often set by feedback from the members (in the broadest sense). Companies are very rarely democracies, yet they may well benefit from an attempt in this direction.

One way to gather input from staff/members to form or influence the organisation's strategy is to conduct a survey. Like most forms of communication, and much of democracy in general, this has its flaws and is open to misunderstanding and misuse. Nevertheless, if the right questions are asked in the right sequence of the right people, then useful information can be gathered that would not be available any other way.

Of course organisations do frequently use surveys, typically in marketing, and not so much on strategy as on tuning products and checking customer experience. So what of surveys in change management? They can be very useful to gauge opinions and solicit ideas, and also to create an inclusive ethos where the organisation's staff feel a part of the change rather than having it thrust upon them. The risk of course is in allowing expectations to grow that all opinions will be handled and all ideas used, and this must be mitigated by both the message around the survey and the phrasing of the questions, and also by how the results are made available.

what is a strategic plan?

The *Survey On Change* by Impact Executives referenced in Chapter 1 asked the question in 2012 "Considering the increasing pace of change, do you think 3+ year strategic plans still have genuine business value?" The responses from the 260 business leaders in companies of all sizes was 70% Yes, 30% No. In their summary report (Journal Issue 29 pp 14-17), Impact concluded that "many medium-term strategic plans are a waste of time, yet companies persist with them". Interestingly they also report that "30% of respondents say that half the programmes and projects they put in place to help their companies adapt to change, fail". I can't help wondering if this is the same 30% who don't think 3+ year strategic plans have any value?

Let's just think for a moment what people might be meaning by a '3+ year strategic plan'. If by this they mean a vision, or mission, then that is not a strategy. If they mean a set of statements of desire with no grounding in achievability, risks and options, then that is not a strategy. Too often the term 'strategy' is simply taken to mean 'high-level', with a sub-text of 'don't bother me with the (uncomfortable) details'. The term 'strategic plan' is a misnomer, because what we mean to say (I hope) is a plan for defining and executing the strategy. A strategy is an interconnected set of observations, analyses, communications, options, decision points, and actions. It is far more than a simple statement of aims.

I do not disagree with Impact's view on the value of many organisations' medium term, so-called strategic plans. Still, let's not infer that we can do away with medium-term strategies altogether, due to the increased pace of change. My assertion is instead that organisations need proper strategies more than ever, to act as frameworks for action, and because developing a strategy is a test of the achievability and risks associated with the required outcomes.

Thus part of the test of a strategy is whether we can make an action plan to execute it that is believable and achievable. If not, this suggests a review of the strategy, and around we go again.

illustration: supplier management

In most changes there is at least one supplier involved, often they have an ongoing relationship with the organisation, and this relationship is a considerable weakness or risk for the change. With a single supplier for a given facility or service the 'deadly embrace' is formed wherein neither can drop the other because there is too much invested and it would be too disruptive.

So what is the strategy to mitigate this risk, accepting that complete removal of the risk is impractical? I suggest the following four-pronged approach.

Select suppliers that are neither tiny nor huge in comparison to our organisation – if we are overwhelming or insignificant to the supplier, there won't be any balance in the relationship;

Use two competing suppliers with duplicate or overlapping capabilities; this keeps each one honest and competitive, avoiding complacency. The extra overhead of managing them is more than repaid in anything other than the most lethargic of organisations;

Publicise the suppliers' performance, thereby providing a consistent assessment with objective comparison, and a level playing field;

Finally, work on a constructive relationship that is not based upon contractual threats but instead on the mutual benefit that underpins any such relationship, whether that benefit be tactical or strategic, direct or indirect.

keeping it alive

Strategy management does not stop when the change implementation starts, it keeps handling the big picture until the change is done and the outcome benefits are measured.

The time of highest risk to a strategy is in the middle period of implementation, when the initial adrenaline has worn off and yet the end goals are still some way off. If complacency sets in a small drift may not be properly assessed, leading to a much bigger correction later.

The ways to mitigate this include: establishing trust early on between all stakeholders and participants; understanding incentives of all stakeholders and participants, and managing misalignments promptly;

encouraging continuous communication; watching like a hawk for deviations that may go outside the strategy framework, or alterations in external factors.

I finish this section with a reference to John Kay's book *Obliquity*, whose basic tenet is that many goals are more likely to be achieved when pursued indirectly. Broadly speaking I interpret this personally as advice to do what you enjoy, and because you enjoy it you will do it well, and this will lead to recognition and success more effectively than if you aim directly for success (however you define that). Kay refers to Buffett and Soros, those legendary investors, describing financial acumen as navigating successfully through many irresolvable uncertainties. We could consider that managing change in an organisation is akin to this observation, yet one thing is certain: Buffett and Soros have a strategy and they stick with it, they keep it alive; it deals with their known unknowns, and when the unknown unknown arises they use tactics to remain within their strategy. We should do exactly the same.

Tactics are temporary

Tactics are usually short-lived actions and outcomes, to support or defend the strategy. They may appear contrarian when viewed in isolation, and that may be part of their mechanism. Sometimes they are pre-meditated, and sometimes they are reactions to situations that arise. Occasionally they take the form of a trade-off, as in "if I adjust this, you agree to do that".

try stuff out

Watch out for paralysis by analysis – there is such a thing as too much thinking and planning. In some circumstances, where the risks and adverse consequences are low, it may be right to just do stuff and see what happens. This is a tactical approach to try stuff out and tidy it up later when we find what works.

When there is sufficient uncertainty in the requirements, practicality or sustainability of a change, then a formal pilot project is called for. This might be as small as a 'laboratory experiment' under controlled conditions that simply lets stakeholders and customers see and feel the possibilities. Or it might be a full implementation but in a very small, controlled instance where the impact of retreating is acceptable.

contrary action

An example of contrary action for a bigger picture in normal life is tactical election voting. Our strategy is to see party A get elected. In our particular constituency their biggest national rival, party B, is the strongest candidate, closely followed by party C and then party A far behind. If just following our strategy, we would vote for A, yet that probably would have no effect in our constituency. Instead if we place a tactical vote for C we might block B and therefore reduce our party rival's success.

Here is a less convoluted, and less contrary, example that I have used in an organisation at the beginning of an assignment. Create a simple diagram on one A3 sheet with big fonts and plenty of white space, showing the change that is going to happen. Take it round to senior management and all stakeholders with a short list of simple questions to tease out their understanding, support, worries, or downright antipathy. It may be that the change is not negotiable, and it may be that we know in advance what their input is likely to be. The tactic is that by doing this we are ensuring they feel involved, we are opening up the communication channels, and we are starting to build trust on a personal basis. Just beware of making too many promises.

trades

If we are involved in constructing a trade-off, the sweet spot is to find something that is higher value to the receiver than the giver, or at least can be presented in that way. It works even if both parties are aware of this. We need to ensure that everyone 'saves face', or that in one way or another everyone is a winner.

In an example of this, I was having difficulty in negotiating a change in working practices with trade union representatives. They could not agree to alter the locations where staff took their rest breaks, despite understanding how this fitted into the bigger changes. Informally I asked if there were other related issues outstanding that we might include in the discussions, and discovered a long-simmering resentment about insufficient storage and microwave facilities causing staff to queue to prepare their food. I proposed a considerable expansion of these facilities in the new locations, whereas it had been impractical previously, and the union was able to present this to their members as a win-win – all it cost management was a few microwaves, with the added benefit of happier staff.

Two-way communications

This is a good time to talk about communications generally, and emphasise their crucial and central role in managing change.

I want to emphasise the benefits of ensuring the two-way nature of all communication. Yes, the main direction of structured information and instruction is from the managers and the planners to everyone else who is involved. There are also tremendous potential benefits in questions, suggestions and information flowing from everyone into the managers and planners. I call the route for this a 'back channel', and for every communication and for the whole life of the change (and indeed for BAU) there should always be a number of back channels that are open, continuously monitored, and acted upon promptly

Socialising change using the internet and mobile technologies is all the thing now. In fact we have been socialising change for decades, in a patchy manner, we just didn't call it that. A decade ago it was all email, but two decades and more ago there were printed memos and notices on notice boards (the sort that hung on the wall). Oh, and meetings where everyone crowded into a single room. The back channel then for solicited and unsolicited input was a physical suggestions box and a pile of blank forms.

There is no doubt that today we have many more tools, compared to previous generations. But are we prepared, do we have the capability, to use them effectively – or do we make the same old mistakes, magnified by the lens of the media?

communities and channels

The commonly used phrase 'global village' is misleading. It purports to mean that we are all connected now, through the accelerating communication facilities invented over the last century from broadcast radio and television to private computer networks and the public internet. In a village we have common knowledge and common purpose, along with rumour and power plays as in any human community, and we know who people are, how they fit in and their family and business history – in other words we have a huge amount of context with which we can interpret the words and actions at any particular time. Our global village, so-called, is missing all the context until we build it up with individual trusted connections. The commonality of knowledge and purpose is also at risk because it is all too easy to fake it when not face to face. So beware.

It is advisable to create and encourage communities both off-line and on-line (physical and virtual). People like communicating in a safe environment, when they have a sense of belonging and familiarity.

This is a list of all the different communications channels I have used in the past. Perhaps you can add some that I have missed:

- daily briefing on intranet
- email
- messaging
- video
- teleconference
- videoconference
- website
- online forum
- text database eg Sharepoint
- broadcast voicemail
- ecalendar
- printed newsletter
- noticeboard
- flyers & poster
- management meeting
- conference
- town hall meeting

Meetings are best used to establish shared knowledge, understanding, actions and responsibility, and to encourage and reinforce that feeling of inclusion and belonging.

Here is my ideal structure for a Change Microsite on the organisation's intranet:

- high-level information on the Change in context of the whole organisation
- high-level plan of timescales and deliverables
- news and progress

- call for testers, local champions and other relevant involvement
- contact details and webforms inviting questions and suggestions

It is helpful to construct an Identity - a brand, logo, or tagline that is used in all communications, because people become familiar with this over time, and familiarity is a first step towards trust.

I recommend that we draw up a matrix of stakeholder communities, both functional areas and staff groupings (seniority), versus communication channels. Then mark onto the matrix for each target community the channels and back channels to be used. Include timings and frequency if appropriate. It is particularly important to keep websites, forums and noticeboards refreshed and up to date. Information that is even slightly out of date will generate unnecessary questions and lose trust.

messages

The KISS principle: I recall an introduction to KISS very early in my working life by a stubbly manager with an Einstein hairstyle - it was a bit of a shock. "Keep It Simple, Stupid" he would roar at me in a thick Glaswegian accent, and of course he was right. We might remove the invective and call it KIS.

The point is that it's easy to embrace (unlike him) yet surprisingly hard to do - we live apparently in a sea of complexity. Part of a Change Manager's job is to manage that complexity and stop it disturbing the high-level simple view of the vision, the realisable benefits, and the roadmap from here to there to which all stakeholders can sign up. It doesn't matter if you are not designated as a change manager – this is relevant for everyone who works around them.

The next segment below talks about tailoring the message, and indeed the back channel, to each different audience. We must generate consistent messages told in different ways to suit the recipients, and delivered through different channels.

In all communications it helps to show the connectedness of people's daily actions to the grand plan, the big picture, and the organisation's raison d'etre.

Never quote one instance of something – it is the majority and the trend that is the measure. One instance is only an illustration of a trend at best, it is not a trend indicator and may be a misleading outlier or exception.

We may not always be able to reach our audience directly. Sometimes our message needs to be relayed through an intermediary. The obvious example is translation into a different language. Another possibility is the need to deliver it as a spoken presentation to many locations around the world, requiring local presenters. A not uncommon need is for delivery by the immediate manager; this is a person the audience is more likely to trust than a stranger who has jetted in from head office. In very large organisations there may even be a cascade down many levels of management. In such situations, beware of message dilution: how far does it go before it loses its impact, how many levels of management. One way to guard against this is to engage directly with local champions who are our eyes and ears 'in the field'. The ideal champion is someone who has the ability to look at the change from our point of view, and help to translate that into the local context and language.

speak for the listener

Self-awareness is the key to having optimal spoken communication. It is very helpful if we can be thinking about how we are coming across at the same time as we are speaking. This means observing our audience and responding to what we see and hear. This requires a dual track in our head, observing and speaking at the same time, which is not easy and requires some practice.

'Speak for the listener' is my phrase that means we should use the language, style, speed, rhythm and even pitch that is most easily heard and understood by our audience. It is always too tempting to talk about something using our own language, to describe from our own viewpoint, because that is easier. This is all the more true if we are nervous, uncertain or in a rush. Unless the audience is our immediate group or direct peers, they will not understand us properly, they will not relate or feel any sense of belonging to our delivery, and that precious thing called trust will fly out of the window.

Speaking for the listener requires us to figure out their viewpoint and be familiar with their language and how they talk about the subject in hand. This is an excellent discipline, although it is not always easy. Delivering in this way subliminally generates the impression that "she understands where we are coming from, and I recognise and feel a part of the subject under discussion". As well as encouraging trust, and a positive spiral of constructive attitudes, this approach increases the likelihood of good questions.

In a sense we are being a chameleon – adapting to the context, not to hide but to avoid frightening or confusing people and so be a more effective communicator.

Some people hate the Q&A session that generally comes at the end of a talk or presentation. I have known people to deliberately overrun their talk so there is no time for it. This is a mistake. The Q&A time is another opportunity for people to feel involved, to make it one big 'us' rather than the old 'us and them'. Questions are to be encouraged, even to the extent of ensuring there is someone willing to ask the first question to get the ball rolling. Of course we need to answer the questions succinctly and openly. In my view it is far better to say "I don't know the answer to that, so I will ensure everyone receives an answer by [date]", than to pretend to know the answer by rambling on.

There is one more communication principle that I espouse. Demystify the subject at every opportunity. Don't dress things up, break them down. I'm not suggesting we over-simplify to the point of losing the message of course. It is a matter again of judging our audience and the level of detail or complexity that they need to hear, in order to achieve what we want from the delivery.

It is worth noting that the principles discussed here apply equally to written communication as they do to verbal.

document management

I have a few things to say on this rather mundane subject, and I'll get it over with quickly. I am not talking about document content, I am talking about how we organise documents and make them accessible to others. If this is not done well, it is another way in which people can feel excluded, can generate an excuse for inaction, or can do the wrong thing.

So when deciding on the structure of a library of folders, here are my recommendations:

- structure for the reader not the author – think about how people will look for things
- structure for deliverables not actions – deliverables are firm, actions are negotiable
- use the same structure in all different areas: online file directory; physical folders; email folders; web pages or favourites (if applicable); RACI matrices (see Chapter 5, **Management & team**)
- never send files in emails, instead send a link to the single, version-controlled copy of the file – that way people save the link and always look at the latest version of the file

---

digression: documents in present tense

Documents that are hard to read do not get read. Complex grammar and sentence structure makes text hard to read. Many documents are written before a change is implemented, and all of them are written before it is completed. Consequently the documents are typically written in the future tense, because that is how the author is thinking about it at the time of writing. However the document will be read before, during and after the change is implemented, and reading the future tense after the fact is rather confusing. Further, documents that comment on or constrain the other documents or the work itself, such as quality manuals, are often written in the future tense using 'shall', as in "the governance committee shall meet monthly".

There is a simple answer to all of these issues. Write documents in the present tense, using the simplest grammar possible. In my experience this causes no problems and makes the documents considerably more accessible to everyone.

One other thing while I'm on documents: every document of any type must have in it the filename, version, date and author, with version and page number/identifier on every page – no exceptions.

---

good news, bad news

It is worth stating the obvious here, which is that things do go wrong and there are times when bad news has to be delivered. Everyone (well, almost everyone) understands that. What makes a difference in the effectiveness of managing the news is the timing and style of delivery.

If you have bad news to deliver, I have two different recommendations. The first is to deliver it as early as possible. Don't sit on it, because it might leak out in an uncontrolled manner. However bad it is, it always looks better if we are on top of it. The second is to roll up different pieces of bad news and deliver it all at once. Bad news causes a reaction that has to be managed, and the size of the reaction does not necessarily reflect the size of the bad news. In any case, it is better to have one big reaction than a series of smaller reactions, because it takes less time to clear the air and regain a positive mindset.

These two suggestions might seem to be contradictory, to which I say "that's life". Real life and real management is often about the art of choosing the best compromise for the situation. So we might choose to anticipate further bad news to achieve a 'roll up', or we might decide there is sufficient recovery time between bad news deliveries that we can afford multiple events. Certainly I have been known to go to the Board and report "this has gone wrong, and there's a strong likelihood that will go wrong soon; my proposal to respond to both is xxx".

Turning to good news, which of course we expect to report far more often, I have a different recommendation. Deliver it as 'little and often' as you can. A continuous plateau or better still a rising slope of positive information is far more beneficial to the mindset than the occasional euphoric peak separated by an information void.

the Kis n Tell approach

This is about Keeping It Simple and Telling (communicating) it well. Then people will understand it, or feel they do, and are more likely to support it. If the message is complex and/or lengthy they are much less likely to understand it and will therefore be more likely to criticise it.

Of course change is rarely simple, there is always complexity. Most people do not need to know all the complexities; they need to know what is relevant to them, with suitable context, explained in terms with which they are familiar. It is part of any manager's job, and especially the change manager, to contain the complexity. Don't let people think something is "complicated", because that is a pejorative term suggesting they cannot or will not do it. Create a framework of simplicity, within which are pockets of complexity that are handled by the right people rather than worried about by everyone.

It is easy to forget, as a manager, that by the time we communicate a change to our people, we have generally had anywhere from a few weeks to a few months to get our head around it. And then we expect our staff, on first hearing, to be as accepting of the change as we now are after much thought and questioning. So it's important to do a number of things in the communication process: handle perceived negatives early; handle real negatives honestly; provide multiple public and private channels for responses; handle all responses constructively and manage expectations; allow time for this process before taking the next step.

There is a further point here, which is that as a manager we have access to a wider context about the change – our staff have a narrower horizon of information and awareness. Belonging is a natural human trait, and change threatens that. So it's important that we provide that broader context for them, so they see how they belong to this change and the new structure/role/process that is the outcome, and how it belongs to them.

Going back to this chapter's opening story, Olaf the project manager clearly has a challenging communication task on his hands, and needs help from both Carla and Mohammed. He has to confess to the lack of strategic oversight in a way that minimises the loss of trust in his Operations Director and his department. He has to re-assert the internal benefits of the change whilst acknowledging all the other factors that have affected it. He has to focus on the external (customer) benefits of the change whilst explaining away the apparent downsides, providing a path through to acceptance.

communicating trust

In Chapter 2 we talk about trust as part of the organisation ethos that helps change. The big question is how to establish that trust. From my experience I recommend the following framework when starting up a significant change project, which is adaptable to each individual circumstance:

- the change is led & facilitated by a high-profile individual who is outside the organisation's operational management; they may be someone assigned from within the organisation, or they may be an external practitioner or even an investor – the important point is that this change manager is experienced, dedicated, very visible, with no conflicts of interest; if they are *not* a subject matter expert in the organisation's business then they are *better* able to challenge and to pose the 'dumb' questions without blinkers or assumptions or historical/emotional baggage, and they can better act as an independent 'sense-checker' that the big picture is understandable by all
- there is open consultation throughout the organisation, even if the senior stakeholders (executive management & investors) already believe there is only one practical option; this starts to break down the "us and them" mindset, and just might provide extra insights from inside the organisation – at all stages there is a clear channel for any staff to raise constructive questions or suggestions, with responses provided swiftly and positively, and a clear understanding of the various timescales

- the senior stakeholders define a clear statement of their vision for the outcome and the expected high-level impacts and benefits – purely the 'what & why' without addressing the 'how, who, where & when' – this is communicated across the whole organisation
- this statement is expanded into a detailed business case that identifies all the different business approaches that could be taken, and examines the consequences of each measured against the expected benefits, and justifies the selected approach; the 'do nothing' option must be included to show the consequences of inaction
- the business case is summarised for each group of people in the organisation in a way that aligns with their interests and incentives, again being open to feedback, so that each group can identify their role in achieving a successful outcome
- there will be occasions where one or more groups are adversely affected; these groups must be honestly briefed before everyone else to manage & contain any disquiet or disruption

If the above is conducted in an honest, open and transparent manner, and if the senior stakeholders listen to the staff, then people will feel they understand the issues and their part in making the change ... even if they don't like it. The implementation can then proceed with a higher degree of confidence and a more predictable timescale.

Upon continued trust we can build mountains.

Takeaways

- creating a strategy starts by asking ourselves, and all stakeholders, all the big questions
- the strategy is maintained from the start until after the change is completed
- strategy protects the change from internal & external pressures, blockers & distractions
- a good strategy acknowledges and deals with challenges, a bad strategy ignores them
- changes to strategy are a big deal, should be rare, and must have top-level sign-off
- clarity of information, thinking, communication, and action - this is how we stay sane
- tactics are developed as circumstances arise, to support or defend the strategy
- tactics are alterable and disposable, and may be reactive or proactive
- all communications must be two-way, with everyone having a channel to provide input
- speaking for the listener ensures that a message is understood in the right context
- establishing trust relies heavily on the right communications at the right time

5 Differing Dynamics

It is a dark and stormy night – suddenly a cry rings out in the gloomy, deserted, open-plan office.

Tony (crouched over his desk, speaking out loud to no-one): aaagh, I need to get home to my Pilates class, I can't finish this Data Report now!

Alex (from a small pool of light across the room): hey Tony, still at it? Didn't I hear you promise Veronica you'd have it on her desk by 9am tomorrow?

Tony: yeah, well, that was last week – I'm stuffed now because the IT people didn't deliver the data until this afternoon, and it's still in a right mess

Alex (strolling across to where Tony is sitting): so what is it you're trying to do here anyway – I mean, I heard there was this huge change going to happen with how we handle all the customer data, but surely that'll take months rather than weeks?

Tony: no it's not a huge change ... well, I suppose there is quite a bit to it. You see, our customer satisfaction survey last year showed they were pretty unhappy about our support response times – so someone up the tree decided we should change our system so we can see the customer history within 5 seconds, while we're on the phone. Thing is, we started by making lots of little tweaks to the old system and no-one actually measured how it was performing before we started, and it looks like it's impossible to reach a 5 second response time, and now we don't know whether we've made enough of an improvement and there's this big review meeting tomorrow morning and ... (voice tails off)

Alex: huh, so you can't go forward, can't go back! You'd best email Veronica with a status summary and go home – stretch your body and give your mind a rest - I reckon the next couple of days could be interesting and you'll need to be on top form, won't you!

Tony: that's alright for you to say but I don't like to break a promise at the last minute (sighs) oh hell, you're probably right 'cos I'd only be delivering something half-cocked and they're probably going to change direction anyway. (sits back) So how come you're here this late anyway, I thought your stuff was all under control?

Alex (smiling ruefully): ha, I'm just tidying up my files because I'm starting something else tomorrow

Tony: oh (pause) what happened?

Alex: I opened my big mouth is what. We had our programme planning review meeting with the top brass last month and it was all very complicated – I mean, changing our procurement processes and contracts across 23 countries is huge – and the benefits didn't seem very clearly defined.

Tony: (drily) you surprise me

Alex: no, really, it's not usually this bad. Anyway I'm just the quality geek, right, but they asked for people's ideas ... so I said what about looking at the impact if we do nothing. There was this silence and then the CEO barked at me "Elaborate!", so I said stuff about the full solution is not always the optimal one, and impacts can be handled in different ways. Then the Finance Director, who never likes spending money, supported me and said he thought there ought to be a review of smaller or later options that would have a clearer cost/benefit ratio with lower risk. And a few weeks later, blow me, they've decided to do nothing until next year, so there's nothing for me to quality assure.

Tony: I reckon you did a good thing, these huge changes usually get bogged down and then circumstances alter and they never deliver – tell you what, I've missed my Pilates anyway by now. Let's go and have a beer to say goodbye to your old project and hello to your new one. We can take a company umbrella, as long as one of us is in early tomorrow to return it.

It is helpful to understand the nature of the change, as well as understanding the content, the players and the pressures. Changes may be far-reaching or very contained, they may be delivered in one big event or bit by bit, they may be driven from inside or outside the organisation. In some of these dynamics we may have options to choose, in others it is a given. Understanding the dynamics helps us to assess the incentives, get the governance right, tune the communications, and build the trust. In this chapter we start with some definitions and go on to some instructions and strong advice.

The above fiction illustrates many aspects of the dynamics of change. There is confusion over the drivers for and scale of change, a lack of planning and measurement, distrust of management, and a little bit of speaking truth to power that opened up a surprising option.

Everyone from guru to graduate tells us, and has been telling us for decades, that "the only constant is change" and "the pace of change is ever increasing" and "the need for change is continuous". Yet the whole point of a change is to move from one 'steady state' to another 'steady state', the latter representing some kind of demonstrable improvement.

The defining ethic in the modern workplace is more, bigger, faster. More information than ever is available to us and the speed of every transaction has increased exponentially, prompting a sense of permanent urgency and endless distraction. Frankly, this is not healthy, and it provides a shield of excuses for poor productivity and change failures. It is true we have more information and therefore more choices than ever before. The proper response is to be smarter about selecting and making those choices.

How organisations manage change

The discipline of 'change management' is a broad church that covers everything from continuous improvement to corporate re-structuring, and it embraces all stakeholders, internal and external.

We must recognise that the desirable status of an organisation is the steady-state operation that is profitable (in whatever terms are relevant to the business). Significant change moves the organisation from one steady-state to another, better-performing steady-state, whereas incremental change fine-tunes that steady-state via small and reversible adjustments.

Confusion over terminology could defeat us at the outset, so let me set out my stall on this. I have already included some terms in the Terminology section at the back of the book, including 'project' which I use as a generic for the function, or set of activities, that delivers a change. My strong view, and I am far from alone in this, is that a project size and scope must be restricted to that which can be understood at a detailed level by one individual, the project manager. It follows that anything other than a small change requires multiple projects, and they must be co-ordinated; this is the function of the 'programme'. This diagram shows my view of the standard relationships between change (in grey) and the normal operation, in any organisation.

Standard relationships

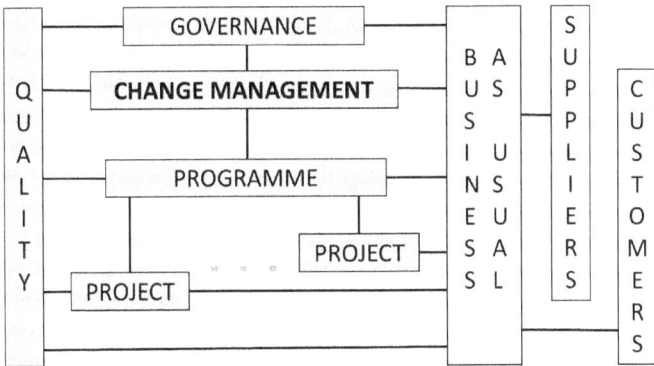

The role of 'governance' is to provide sponsorship, strategic direction and monitoring, and an escalation path for major risks and issues that cannot be handled within the project or programme.

Alongside all of this delivery activity is usually a responsibility called 'quality' which defines and monitors standards, procedures and good practices throughout the organisation.

The 'customers' are those within, and sometimes outside, the organisation who requested, or are affected by, the change. They are hooked in at all levels in a two-way relationship.

Change Management covers everything in this diagram, including the eventual effect within the organisation and its relationships with the rest of the world. A Change Manager role is typically positioned at the programme or governance level, and is accountable for the effectiveness of the change.

---

digression: change control

Change Management and Change Control can easily be confused in people's minds. This book is about the realm of Change *Management*, i.e. managing a required or desired change from inception to wrap-up. Change *Control* on the other hand is the tactical process of handling changes that arise <u>within</u> a planned and committed activity; this may be within the regular operation or within any project activity.

The purpose of Change Control is to handle changes to agreed deliverables such that the impact and consequence of each change, and the cumulative effect of many changes, is fully evaluated and understood before that change is authorised (or mitigated, or denied).

Change Control is an important process. No matter how well a project is planned and how well the requirements are defined, there will always be requests to change something about the project, usually in the product being delivered. There are good reasons for this: the business does not stand still while our project is progressing so we expect that the ongoing business will trigger the need for small changes to the products and services being built to support that business. If we do not do this, then our project risks delivering something that is out of date on day one.

Four-way tension

In any change there is a four-way tension between time, cost, function and quality. This has to be prioritised and managed on a per project basis. There will almost always be the need for flexibility within the organisation as the change is executed. The more that is thought through in advance, and the better that expectations are communicated and managed, the better the responses and the lower the stress.

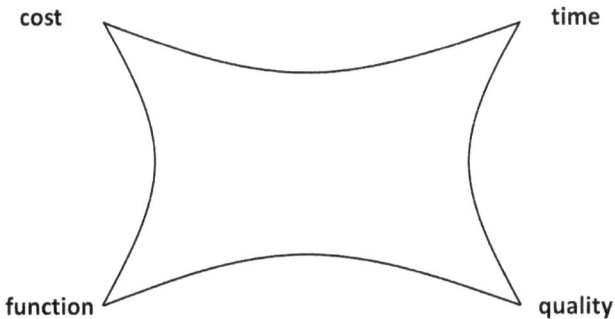

cost   time

function   quality

This diagram shows a 'stretched blanket' held by different generic factors at the four corners. If any one of these factors is altered it pulls the blanket and affects the other three. Although this might appear to be technology related, it is relevant to any deliverable outcome. For instance, reducing the time available for the change, because the benefits are needed earlier, is not an uncommon situation. Whatever this does to cost, it certainly compromises either function or quality, and difficult trade-offs may need to be made. Evaluating those trade-offs may need research and analysis, for which more time is needed, and then we have come full circle – unless this was anticipated before the change started. So it's a good discipline at the outset to conduct what-if tests on adjusting these factors.

Of the four factors, 'time' is the most outwardly and immediately visible, the one that can gain or lose trust very easily ... and trust leverages many things as we discussed earlier. I am a great believer in maintaining 'time' above all else. The date we deliver something is very visible, and may have all sorts of interdependent links to other activities. Olympic Parks are a good example of this; every 4 years there are cost overruns, certain peripheral functions may be missing or late, and sometimes we worry about the quality ... but they have to deliver the main functions on time, and cost takes the biggest hit.

Range & scale

People often don't recognise significant or 'paradigm' change, mistaking it for step or incremental change, for three reasons. They don't see it; their frame of reference is too small for them to see the bigger picture, the broader effect, perhaps even the true cause and effect. They don't recognise it; they have insufficient experience, imagination or open-mindedness to understand or acknowledge what they see. They don't believe it; this may be scepticism about the achievability or sustainability, or it may be denial born out of vested interest in maintaining the status quo.

Worse than this, people don't see a change at all or the need for it, due to being conditioned to only look for what they expect to see. The ability to see beyond the horizon and be open to new 'noises' or 'movements', and the ability see connections between apparently separate entities, actions and scenarios is something that all managers should strive for, and certainly marks out the change professional.

We have talked about the importance of a change 'handing over' effectively to BAU or the normal operation. This may indeed be a 'big bang' where BAU goes through a huge step change at one time, for instance an organisation moving into a new building over a weekend. Often, though, the change delivery into BAU happens at various points during the project, even to the point of acting like a drip-feed every week. In my experience, an example of the latter would be business process change in an airline or airport.

The following segments identify different ranges and scales of change. I use the simple analogy of paddling a canoe along a river to illustrate the differences.

incremental change

'Continuous change' is a phrase that is bandied around by executives and commentators almost as a badge of honour. To my mind, if we are continuously changing that can suggest that we are behind the game, or don't even know what the game is, and can lead to a rolling 'benefits tomorrow' syndrome where no benefits are ever delivered.

What I think people really mean is that they are continuously open to making changes, in response to opportunities and threats, in this ever faster world. They mean continual rather than continuous – a small yet vital difference.

There is a genuine form of continual change, more properly called continual improvement, or incremental change, which looks continuous from a distance. This is where methodologies like Six Sigma come in, and it is particularly applicable to an operation where the same sequence of actions are repeated. Examples are in manufacturing, logistics, and call centres. The changes are in the form of tuning to achieve better efficiency and quality, and responsibility for them is delegated way down in the organisation.

There is a canoe analogy for this; through practice we adjust our seating position and our arm movement, and even our upper-body strength, to improve the effectiveness of our paddling.

We can make slightly larger changes that are still called incremental if the change is small, non-threatening, and with few if any consequences. If it does not significantly alter the big picture or the overall function within which it occurs. If it is easily reversible, should it turn out to be ineffective or injurious. Although such changes may need scheduling and co-ordination, their effect is still sufficiently local that responsibility for them is delegated from senior project or operational management.

Looking at the canoe analogy, this level of incremental change could be to increase our paddling rate upstream in a faster-flowing section of the river, in order to maintain our overall rate of progress. We might have to slow down later if we are becoming exhausted.

We could argue that incremental is the ideal way to deliver change, because it is non-disruptive and very low risk. Unfortunately it is simply not applicable to the majority of changes because we need to replace or add something, rather than tuning what we already have. That said, it is worthwhile when conducting the solution analysis, ask ourselves how we can make this look like continual or incremental improvement for the customer, because that is when they will be happiest.

step change

A step change is disruptive in some way, and alters some function of the organisation without changing the overall direction. It typically requires careful scheduling, and testing beforehand, because on a specified date we stop doing things this way and start doing them that way.

In the simple canoe analogy, a step change is when we get out of the canoe to drag it past some obstruction. We are still propelling it up river with our own effort, though in a different way as dictated by the circumstances.

A manufacturing example of step-change is where we were selling cars only in black, and now we are going to offer four different colours. On the face of it this is a simple change to the manufacturing line, but it has a lot of consequences. How do we decide which colours to offer? Will we provide the colours to order, or will we do market research to estimate the numbers we need in stock, and how do we handle short-falls or over supply? We will need a five-fold increase in the range of touch-up paint products, with the associated increase in stock costs.

transformational change

Transformative or transformational change is very disruptive and significantly alters the function or direction or attributes of the organisation. Usually this is for the better, although don't ignore the examples of down-sizing and take-overs, which usually have disbenefits for some staff.

Once more in the canoe analogy, a transformational change is to break the accursed paddle across our knee, dump the canoe, buy a sailing dinghy and let the wind do the work. We are still travelling across water, but in a very different way.

tipping point

This is not a scale of change, rather it describes a small step that has large consequences, usually the last step in a sequence or accumulation of steps or actions. The literal example is if we begin lifting an armchair from behind, pivoting on its front feet; at first it requires a lot of effort, then the effort gradually reduces until it is almost balanced – the tiniest push at this tipping point causes the armchair to keep moving until it comes to rest in a different orientation. The suggestion here is to think about where we are on the cycle of change. Are we at the beginning where heavy lifting is required, or are we near the tipping point where a tiny amount of pressure in the right direction will have the desired result? Or is that result too unpredictable so that we need to put some restraining forces in place after the tipping point (analogous to holding the armchair as it comes down to the floor to avoid breaking the coffee table)?

outcome clarity

There's one more way in which we can think about the different nature of the change, and that is in terms of how well-defined the outcome really is. I suggest there are four categories:

- **deterministic** - a well-trodden path, with known outcomes
- **directed** - a well-anticipated path, with defined outcomes
- **constrained** - an unclear path, with desired outcomes
- **exploratory** - no particular path, and unclear outcomes

It is worth thinking through which of these best matches our situation, because then we can manage expectations and activities to best effect.

Looking back at this chapter's story we can see that Tony's project is confused about the scale, whether the outcome can be achieved by incremental adjustments or whether they need at least a step change in how the data is managed. It rather sounds as if there may not even be a project, that the tweaks are being done in an operational context with no planning, and clearly this has run into the sand. Almost certainly this should have been approached as a step change project in the 'directed' category.

Drivers

There are three different angles that may be helpful when thinking about the drivers for a particular change. An understanding of which dynamics best describe our situation does help us to tailor communications, manage risks and prioritise actions.

convergent versus divergent

These are my terms, and I have coined them as a result of experience and analysis across many changes; some as an outside observer, and some where I have been deeply involved. There are important distinctions between convergent and divergent in terms of the factors for successful, sustainable change, especially in incentives, belonging, and outcome measurements.

Convergent change is where the organisation remains largely the same when viewed from the outside. Although the period of change may take the staff away from their 'centre-line', once the change is operational they are back on it. The organisation may end up being larger and with a wider scope, building on its history and investment. An example is where some exploratory project leads to a modification or extension to the product line; the integration into BAU might be a challenge but it's a nice kind of challenge to have. Alternatively an organisation may become smaller or more tightly focused, or 'back to basics' in response to difficult market conditions

Divergent change is where the organisation changes direction or expands into very different activities, or breaks up. The outcome is usually disruptive, with a very different organisation shape and function yet still with existing value to be preserved, such as brand, or plant, or staff expertise. An example here is when private equity takes on a struggling diversified company, sells off some components and merges some with other companies in their portfolio. Another example of divergent change is where a successful organisation uses its brand to start up in an entirely new business; think about Virgin going into aviation, and then banking.

The convergent change, then, requires a focus on minimising disruption, reinforcing the common incentives, presenting the change as evolution, and measuring the expansion or contraction of similar activities. It directly involves only certain groups of staff, with others being briefed as appropriate. The divergent change, in contrast, is deliberately disruptive. It typically requires wholesale preparation with whole swathes of staff who are concerned for their futures both short and long term, and may require the efficient induction and integration of new staff with new knowledge and skills. Incentive management and re-creating a strong sense of belonging must be a top priority, along with defining outcome measurements for success and sustainability that are meaningful in the new paradigm.

---

illustration: convergent unsung hero

A marketing manager for an existing product feels that her bosses are paying less attention as they focus on integrating new products, and she has a reduced budget; this doesn't make her feel good in that local context. On the other hand if part of her annual bonus is based on overall company profits or she's a shareholder in the company, then she anticipates a reward in the future and is more prepared to accept the shorter-term constraints. The deft senior manager will have prepared the ground with her by explaining that the company is crucially reliant on her to continue the success of the current products during this convergent period, while there is a strain on the budget and management bandwidth, and they are confident she will rise to the challenge.

---

mandated versus discretionary

Mandated change is externally driven, the prime examples being new regulatory or legal requirements, or demands from a parent organisation or even a supplier. The choices are typically limited to when and how to make the change.

Discretionary change is an internal decision, entirely within the control of the organisation, and clearly all options are available in principle, including "forget it".

Mandatory changes are in no way easier; they still need a fit-for-purpose vision and all the rigour of change management. They still have options, they still need enrolment (or sign-up, or commitment), perhaps even more so. There is no difference in the challenges of managing incentives and trust.

proactive versus reactive

In broad terms a reactive change is responding to events, whereas a proactive change is anticipating events.

The advantage of being proactive is that we are more likely to have control of, or influence over, various factors, including most importantly the timing. We also have the option of including other related work and thus working more efficiently.

The advantage of being reactive is that we only do what is necessary, and when it is necessary, and so avoid wasting effort anticipating events that do not happen or turn out slightly differently.

As with a lot of change management, there is no clear right and wrong. Rather it is a matter of making the optimal judgements at the optimal time in each situation.

Organisation shapes & styles

There are many variations in how an organisation is structured and the style of its management. Although, again, there is no right or wrong answer, it is helpful to understand some of the main differences as they relate to the ability, readiness and commitment for implementing change. I am not suggesting we are able to alter the whole organisation, unless of course that is part of our change programme's required outcomes.

A real danger for large, poorly co-ordinated organisations is that they eat their own tail without recognising it. In other words the result of some action is to inadvertently injure another part of the organisation. This happens when they are so big that the pain takes a while to register, or they are so hungry they don't recognise the pain.

---

illustration: freedom to innovate

The choices an organisation has in responding to individual staff initiatives can be likened to the toddler in the park with his mum. When the toddler wanders into the bushes I see three responses from the mum. The supportive mum goes in with the toddler, chatting about what they can see and pointing out the dangers of being scratched by twigs. The cautious mum stands at the edge and says "come out of there now, you're not allowed and you'll hurt yourself". The distracted mum is on her mobile phone, facing the other way. Organisations are very like those mums.

---

layers and silos

First we consider the horizontal shapes or layers in a typical organisation chart.

A large organisation that is strongly hierarchical is one with many layers, typically 7 to 10, between the board and the people who produce stuff. The decision-making and approval processes are often laborious and slow, especially where something affects multiple areas, departments or divisions. Stakeholders can be hard to identify and reach, and there may be different management styles in different areas. On the positive side, it is easy to assign accountability and responsibility and there are strong audit trails of discussions and decisions.

A flat organisation has only perhaps 2 or 3 such layers, and it delegates far more decisions and approvals to the lower level of managers and doers. This makes it easier to get decisions and identify stakeholders. On the other hand there are more stakeholders, at a less senior level, and it is harder to manage them and ensure co-operation on a single agenda.

Now let's consider the vertical shapes or pillars in a typical organisation chart.

There are always departmental pillars or columns in an organisation unless it is quite small and simple. This arises from the separation of the activities and the relevant skill sets. It is not practical or desirable for the research director to manage the marketing department, nor for the operations director to run product development. As an aside, there is an interesting exception here in that IT is still often managed by the Finance Director and there has been an ongoing debate for years about whether the IT director should be on the board. I can only think this is an historical hangover from when the payroll was the most important function of IT – and yes, of course the IT director should be on the board because IT underpins almost everything we do, and is only going to increase as an amplifier for the effectiveness of the organisation.

It is therefore often necessary, in any change programme other than something purely local, to reach sideways across department boundaries. Some organisations have vertical separation into silos for historical or political reasons rather than functional or management reasons, and those present extra challenges due to defensiveness and control issues. We can go up, across and down to encourage someone to cooperate.

Although it is far more effective if we can find a way to reach directly across, using existing connections such as IT or HR or even Finance.

Then in addition to the vertical and horizontal dimensions there are geography and culture. If our organisation is multi-national, or has functions outsourced to different cultures and time-zones, this presents further challenges. Everyone is inconvenienced and everyone needs to put in extra effort, to bridge the gaps between times and cultures. We could be scrupulously fair and arrange equal impact on each function or country. Alternatively we could assess the willingness of different functions or countries to accommodate the extra effort, and weight the impact accordingly. That way those who are more happy to adapt are feeling good about doing so, and those less happy to adapt are pleased they got off lightly. Of course those accepting the greater impact must be gently feted as heroes, without overtly criticising others.

management ethos

There are three main styles of management in my view:

- command and control
- negotiation and consensus
- grassroots democracy

The 'old school' version of the first one is "their incentive is to damn well do what I say, or they'll get fired". This still exists, although it is becoming rarer. If encountered, the best response is to knuckle down and accept it, or move on if you don't like it; you probably won't get it changed.

All three styles can work well, regardless of the strength of hierarchy or depth of silos, as long as they are listening to the staff. The most productive style depends on the organisation's history, the activities, the people, and even the external stakeholders. Most organisations blend a combination of all three, with a more enlightened version of command and control as the lead style and taking input from the other two styles, with the overall weighting depending on the circumstances.

Listening or taking input is the key component of a successful management ethos, because staff value the opportunity and often have something valuable to contribute. If this is followed by clear decision-making and direction where the thinking behind it is shared with the staff, then in my experience everyone wins. Of course, this requires competent and confident management.

Imposing change from above is a high-risk approach. If the management and staff are not 'signed up' or 'enrolled' then there are serious dangers of poor implementation, back-sliding and sabotage. Dictatorial regimes tend to suffer from rebellion sooner or later.

---

illustration: Popcorn scenario

An experienced, charismatic, high energy sales & marketing man was put in charge of a new business unit, with a brief to create and sell value adding services on top of the existing data products. He handpicked a team of top performing sales, marketing, product and technical people and myself as programme manager. Initiatives were started and dropped literally on a daily basis, driven by individual egos and agendas, and chaotic discussions. This was truly a lot of popcorn in a small pan – keeping the lid on was difficult. I took on the role of 'organising muscle'.

My first step was to be a friend to each member of the team, to establish some trust and open communication. My second step was to maintain visibility of the expectations and deadlines given by the parent company – wall posters in every room. We then, painfully, agreed a broad set of statements to which everyone could relate, and which defined the short and medium term goals in monetary and

---

market presence terms, the types of third party relationships needed, the acceptable levels of risk and the pitch to the prospective customer base.

The team members then proceeded, led by the boss, to work chaotically exactly as before! The only new thing was the addition of often ingenious rationalisations on how the latest bright idea really did fit into the strategy framework. So I instituted 9am meetings every day, through which all new ideas had to be funnelled, and in which those ideas were 'prioritised'. Only the daft ideas were binned, all others were "put on the list while we concentrate on the top priorities that best deliver against the strategy with lowest risk". Day after day we played the 'game of consequences', pointing out that we cannot do everything, and just occasionally a new opportunity was promoted at the expense of other existing work. Gradually the team became used to the structure and rigour which did not seek to kill their entrepreneurial spirit, but instead helped to channel their energies along optimal paths.

Incidentally we achieved a lot of good work together in the back of a 747 as we shuffled between London and New York – it's the ultimate off-site, no interruptions location (or it was then).

learning & personal development

This is just as important a part of the group of 'support functions' as payroll in Finance, contracts in Legal and the telephone system in IT. There ought to be perfect, natural alignment here between organisation and staff member; both want the person to become more capable, more productive.

Some L&D approaches get in the way of themselves though, by taking a very top-down, deterministic and instructional approach. Recent thinking is much more about focusing on individuals and tailoring a variety of tools and techniques to suit their needs and that of their organisation. This seems right to me, because once said it is obvious. Such tools and techniques include:

- learning (aka training) courses
- coaching
- on-the-job
- knowledge management
- reference material

These are all part of one learning landscape, and should be joined up.

In the first 16 years of the 21st century there has been a considerable evolution in thinking about the methods and effectiveness of learning and personal development. The training course where we attended a physical classroom used to be a reward, a few days away from the rigours of the regular job. Then classroom became a minority method with the evolution to online learning (eLearning). The current thinking is exemplified by the 70:20:10 model championed by Charles Jennings at the *702010Institute.com*. 70:20:10 views development of an individual as occurring through three types of learning activities:

- 70% Experience - day-today tasks, challenges and practice 'on the job'
- 20% Exposure - with and through others from informal coaching, exploiting personal networks and other collaborative and co-operative actions
- 10% Education - structured courses.

The total Return on Investment (ROI) from effective, integrated learning is never easy to measure quantitatively. It includes these four areas:

- objectives achievement
- reduced lead times on new activities

- money saved from less classroom usage
- staff retention and morale

Naturally we can point people at a course, or any learning experience, but we cannot make them learn. They need the incentive of improved work satisfaction and genuine advancement opportunities, an understanding of the context, a great experience, and appropriate measurement.

People roles

Here I want to draw three different comparisons between types of role. These are all important in understanding the dynamics and relationships inside and outside a change programme team.

permanent v. contract

'Permanent' is something of an outmoded term, in that it comes from an era where 'jobs for life' or working for one organisation throughout our career, or until we chose to move, was common. This is no longer the case, and 'permanent' simply refers to the employment status where the contract is open-ended and the employer is responsible for managing tax deductions and providing statutory benefits such as holiday pay, sick pay, maternity/paternity leave and pension scheme.

'Contract' is an umbrella term for anyone who is not a 'permanent' employee. There are many terms or descriptions under this umbrella, used differently in different industries and situations, and often overlapping or blending into each other. Here are my definitions.

A **Freelancer** is someone working for themselves, rather than as part of a service organisation; it describes the individual. All the following roles describe the individual's relationship with the organisation where they are working; they may be freelancers or they may be provided by another organisation.

A **Temp** is usually hired for their effort, rather than their skills or experience. Typically the role requires little or no training and is low-level and tightly managed.

Interim v. Consultant v. Contractor

The distinction between these terms is an old chestnut. I have read many different views on this, but the distinctions are clear in my mind so I'll share them:

- a contractor works inside the organisation and does as they are told – they are usually hired for their skills
- an interim works inside the organisation, using (or creating) the organisation's methodology and language, and makes things happen using their own skills and experience
- a consultant works outside the organisation, using consultancy methodology and language, and provides the benefit of their experience and wisdom

Is Transformation Change better achieved by permanent or contract staff? The short answer is that we need both interim/consultant and employee components to manage and deliver a change that is transformational (as opposed to incremental, small-scale or functional change). The best combination depends on the individual organisation's situation.

The interim's role crucially includes asking the unaskable, challenging assumptions, facilitating new thinking and, of course, driving hard to deliver the business benefits, unencumbered by politics or promotion prospects. The permanent roles inevitably include high-level sponsorship & budget allocation, operational & infrastructure support, and ongoing ownership.

sponsor v. stakeholder

The most successful, sustainable changes are achieved through a positive, trusting partnership between senior manager(s) and the change manager.

Let's demystify this business of 'stakeholder'. Like so many management terms it has taken on an aura of quasi-religious intensity in recent years. The term stakeholder simply refers to anyone who is likely to be affected by the change. This includes much more than just those who benefit, which is the narrow usage of the term, and much more than just senior management. It includes anyone and everyone for whom the change may have some lasting effect. Once we have a comprehensive list or map of stakeholders, we can create a communication plan that accommodates their numbers and roles. The next step, before doing any communication, is to understand the incentives of the different stakeholders. This is easy to say and can be a hugely difficult task to do properly. Yet to assume, or guess, or worse still ignore it, is to risk everything. Not just that some communication might be ineffective, but that the whole change may fail spectacularly.

The Sponsor on the other hand is a single person, or possibly a small committee, with sufficient seniority to own the change project, ensure it is practically achievable and defend it against other competing projects.

change manager v. the rest

The Change Manager (CM) is agnostic on the quality of the commercial rationale for the change, although they may (should) say something if it seems to them that the strategy is driving towards a cliff. This is more easily achieved when the CM is an interim, as discussed already in **permanent v. contract**. What they do need is a thorough *understanding* of the rationale, in order to manage the communication and structuring of the change.

The CM does not need to understand or be able to do the detail of the business – they do need to understand the high-level constraints, dependencies, opportunities, strengths and weaknesses of the business.

The CM must question, challenge and play devil's advocate to tease out the vision, the expectations, the deliverables, dependencies and risks. This is often best done by someone outside the senior management team, even from outside the organisation. It is better that they are not seen as a subject-matter expert, because they must ask the 'dumb' questions and in some cases they must 'say the unsayable'. This is harder for a member of the permanent staff than it is for an interim, even if they pre-arrange immunity – it's like being an internal whistle-blower.

Any change needs people who are comfortable in the face of uncertainty, as change that is highly predictable is a rare thing. The certainty that saves everyone's sanity comes from using a tried and tested approach and framework within which the new thing is tackled. So we need a healthy mix of creative types and structured types.

People can alter themselves ... a little. However it's what people *are* that can make or break a change. A Change Strategist takes a panoptic approach to all aspects of a change, starting with the question "is this the optimal change for the organisation at this time?"

illustration: hit the ground running

The phrase "hit the ground running" in business means the alternative to an induction period, where the new arrival is passive for days or even weeks. The experienced interim, who is typically and deliberately over-qualified for the role, is active from day one, because they know the things to look for and the questions to ask. This can also apply to an employee who is assigned to a different area of the organisation. I do this using three components: I arrive as prepared and briefed as possible (on the whole organisation not just the role or division); I am quick-witted, adaptable, good-humoured and a good observer of people (crucial to speaking the organisation language and gaining early trust); I have in my mind a lean toolbox of industry standards, good practices and techniques that have worked before, to be deployed sensitively as required and at the right moments.

Management & team

This is not referring to The Organisation within which you work, but rather to how you go about organising (managing) yourself and the team to good effect. It is worth referring back to the simple diagram at the beginning of this chapter that shows the generic relationships between the different management areas during a change.

The Change Team needs to be connected to, yet insulated from, the BAU operation – select your people carefully: advocates, risk-takers, experimenters, champions, negotiators.

Think about the scale of the change, the influence levels of the senior stakeholders, and the size of the team. When the size of the problem is much greater than the influence or capability of those who address it, frustration and chaos usually follow.

Just as an organisation needs both a rigorous and disciplined approach to product quality and incremental changes, and a free-ranging, no-rules area where new ideas can be tried and innovation encouraged, so too does a significant change programme need both of these mindsets. If the whole thing is run in an innovation mindset there will be surprises and disappointments that always arise from such approaches, and the programme will be unpredictable in time, cost, quality and output, something that is rarely acceptable to the stakeholders. On the other hand if the whole thing is run in a rigid and highly structured fashion then the strong likelihood is that innovative solutions to problems will be missed due to straight-line thinking and over-strong governance.

cells or trees

Broadly there are two ways the team can be structured – in a tree or in cells.

The tree has a multi-level hierarchy, it is a familiar structure, people can see where they fit in with everyone else, and responsibility and authority can be moved up and down the tree as necessary. On the other hand it can be quite hard, and confusing for people, to change the tree, and communication can get slowed down or blurred as it moves up and down.

The cell approach is a flatter structure and much more flexible. Cells may be long-lived or short-lived, depending on the responsibility or task assigned to them. People will identify strongly with their cell, although they may be much less clear about the purpose of other cells and how they relate to their own.

Almost all work breaks down into individual tasks with interfaces between them. This is true whether the work involves technology, processes or management. Whatever approach is taken with the structure, the interfaces are more important than the tasks. If we can define and maintain clear interfaces, then the tasks have some freedom as to how they are achieved as long as they conform to the interface. This is true both in terms of developing the content of the change, and operationally after the change has been delivered.

project mechanisms

There are countless books on how to organise projects and the tools to use. In this segment I simply give you a few general observations that might be helpful.

Never be religious or dogmatic about any of these things – remember they are just tools to help us on our way and they must not over-shadow the content of the work they are helping to organise. Make sure the mechanisms and tools are fit-for-purpose, and be pragmatic in their usage.

There are three ways of using a project plan:

- it gives a warm feeling, but ignore it and do knee-jerk actions
- live & die by it, allowing no alterations
- use it as a reference and strong framework, and control variations

and, as you might guess, I always favour the latter.

When looking for a project methodology, in my view almost any methodology will do as long as everyone understands and uses the same one. It saves time by providing a framework for action. It provides a common language for familiarity, shared expectations and efficient communication. It also helps with a sense of purpose, connectedness and belonging. It is much better to adapt a methodology to the situation and people that we have, than to attempt to adapt the people to a strict methodology. Enough said, I hope.

If under-performance or failure generates derision and radical penalties, then they will be hidden, hushed up, and usually get much worse before they are discovered. Much better to encourage openness and treat problems as positive things to be resolved before they become failures.

We need to be inventive to respond to specific challenges in the management process. When I was working alongside a commercial CEO with a highly technical change to implement, I instigated a 15 minute breakfast meeting every day to remind and reset the priorities, and ensure the messages stayed on track.

In Chapter 6 under **Manage Complexity** there are some notes on the provenance and pros & cons of the two main approaches to managing projects, generally described as Waterfall and Agile. Here I simply point you at some publications on mechanisms for the management of change.

The Effective Change Manager's Handbook edited by Richard Smith, David King, Ranjit Sidhu and Dan Skelsey is a 600 page handbook that describes itself as exploring practically the discipline of change management, offering tools, templates and techniques to help the practising change manager perform effectively. From early 2015 it became the official examination guide for the APMG International Change Management qualification, based upon the Change Management Institute's Body of Knowledge and accreditation processes. *Making Sense of Change Management* by Esther Cameron & Mike Green was the previous 'bible' for professional change managers.

Both of these are fine books, yet have their limitations (as do all books, including the one you are reading now). They focus on structure and process, which indeed I espouse myself. They do not focus on the management of the human element. We can follow their instructions perfectly and yet deliver the wrong thing. Just as you could follow the advice in this book and yet employ no structure or methodology at all, and you will get into a mess and fail to deliver.

management

A lack of authoritative management can mean too many people contributing to decisions, leading to compromised and delayed decisions. There is a time for consensus management, and there is a time for command and control. The latter gives people a strong framework within which they can contribute as well as execute, if properly done with plenty of listening.

Empowerment has to be appropriate; if everyone is a leader and a strategist then chaos ensues.

---

digression: managers

In a free-marketeer's perfect world, according to economist Ronald Coase, companies would not exist; we would all be free agents, joining up and splitting apart on a daily basis as required by each new task. But it's hard, for example, to build cars that way because we need planning and co-ordination and decision-making and communication with external groups such as finance, raw materials and delivery. Ants, bees and termites have highly efficient communities without having a management layer; we have some idea how they communicate, yet we don't really understand how they co-ordinate and plan. We don't know how much of their behaviour is innate or instinctive and how much is learned, although I suspect it is mostly the former. Still, they are not at the level of building cars, for which we might be thankful. If they were, it is hard to see how that level of complexity in mutual endeavour could be achieved without some management. Looked at another way, humans are vastly more conscious of 'self' and are easily distracted by 'self' considerations; we're not natural team players, unlike those life-forms that are wholly or primarily instinctive in their actions. So don't shoot the managers; instead give them the responsibility, authority, tools, training and governance structure to ensure they can function effectively and efficiently. Oh, and manage them.

In my view, the ideal strategy team is often three people – led by the change strategist, a highly structured organisational expert, and including a subject matter/industry expert, and a finance expert (because everything always comes down to money in one way or another). I once worked in a strategy team of eight very senior people from different disciplines; it was very productive in terms of ideas and communication, but also like grappling with a hyperactive octopus. The main problem was in getting decisions and making them stick.

RACI for roles

A transformational change, by definition, affects multiple parts of an organisation and is high-profile. This is not achieved by a single individual - a team is required spanning all affected areas and levels of the organisation.

As soon as we have a team we have the scope for confusion over who does what. This is all the more true when we have people with overlapping expertise, differing priorities and multiple involvements in an uncertain situation.

This is where the simple RACI model comes in. The acronym stands for Responsible, Accountable, Consulted, Informed which are the four possible roles someone can have in relation to any kind of deliverable. Accountable is actually the 'highest level' role, although ARCI is a far less pleasant acronym to use (just try saying it):

Accountable - a single person accountable for success
Responsible - people who have actions to deliver
Consulted - people whose input is sought
Informed - people who are told what is happening

Constructing and publishing this simple matrix of names against deliverables can clear up, or better still prevent, a whole load of confusion. We may choose to have a hierarchy of RACI matrices, starting with the high-level outcomes and working down to discreet deliverables or tasks. In deciding where to use it, employ the maxim "if there's likely to be doubt, then spell it out". Remember, as discussed earlier in **two-way communications**, that those in the Informed list must have a channel into the change team to provide input that is not specifically solicited.

Once a RACI matrix is agreed and published, it should not be changed lightly or frequently. Doing so diminishes its authority. Neither is it set in stone. Strong governance is required to ensure that it evolves only when required to suit the situation.

Options for action

Making a successful and sustainable change depends not only on execution and everything that accompanies it before and afterwards, but also on the selection of the optimal changes to which the organisation commits in the first place.

What I mean by optimal changes are those which are practically and politically achievable and which deliver on the organisation's vision with acceptable risk, cost and timescales, and fit-for-purpose quality and function.

A project that does not fit within this framework is either a vanity project or is simply misconceived. In either case it is to be avoided.

If we have the opportunity, and the information available, it is helpful to audit the organisation's history on implementing changes, both successes and failures (and all the partials in between). Look over the last three years and assess the relevance, effectiveness and impact of the changes delivered, and the causes of failure or undershoot for those that did not fully deliver. This gives us an insight into the readiness of the organisation for the next change, and therefore the approach that has the best likelihood of success.

It is often the case that many things need changing in order to achieve the desired end result. This does not mean that all changes should be pursued at the same time; in fact, that approach is almost always a bad idea. Think about priorities, dependencies, quick wins and the capability of the organisation.

In Chapter 3 we discuss the concept of Minimum Necessary Change. This is the time and place to bear this in mind and apply the principles.

none or delay

The no-action or delay-action options must be considered, if only to examine the consequences which may sharpen up the rationales for action. It seems contrarian to suggest that doing nothing is an option, yet if this is discussed and carefully thought through it becomes an excellent test of the necessity for action.

Make sure the conclusions on the (presumably dire) consequences of inaction are recorded in the same document that espouses the vision and translates that into deliverable benefits.

We talk in Chapter 4 about the short-lived actions of tactics that defend the overall strategy. Delaying a change is a not uncommon tactic where time is needed to prepare the ground, or raise the money, or gather the resources, or simply to see if we all still think it is a good idea in three months' time.

analyse & prioritise

The essential advice, especially in a crisis, is to move more slowly and deliberately at the outset, rather than rushing off in a panic. Think quickly and act slowly. The experience of sailing provides metaphors for business, none more so than "hasty fixes cause more problems" (and yes, I do have real scars as evidence of learning).

So armed with a full understanding of the required outcome, and the rationale for it, the next step is to establish and understand the constraints and dependencies, both internal and external, that bear upon the actions. It is helpful, if possible, to gauge this against the contribution each change makes to the big picture.

A set of priorities can then be assigned, which depend upon the circumstances: we might choose to give top priority to the 'biggest win' to reduce the risk of that over-running; or we might choose to prioritise a couple of small 'quick-wins' to show early progress and boost morale. There are many variations, but without the preceding analysis there will probably be some chaos and much disappointment.

We will have people in any or all stakeholder groups saying to us "this preparation is all taking too long, we need to get going". Resisting this in a positive, constructive way is not easy. If possible, have a couple of examples to hand, from within or outside the organisation, where a hasty start has led to trouble. Also have a couple of killer questions that do not as yet have good answers.

Just a word, on the other side of the coin, about 'paralysis by analysis' – it happens to the best of us ... you should have seen me deciding on my new mobile phone contract. The way to avoid it is to accept that decisions are made on the best information available at the time, rather than on perfect information, which is a rare animal. Do not let the analysis become the reason for inaction.

eat the elephant

This popular saying can be useful when faced with a huge change: "how do you eat an elephant? One bite at a time!" In other words, do not be over-awed by the enormity of the task – break the work down into manageable chunks.

The danger in this, of course, is if we are only considering the one bite at any one time. We need someone to be monitoring progress across the whole elephant. There is the old story of the 3 blind men interpreting an elephant as 3 very different animals, because each could only feel one different part of it; we do need the vision, the high-level understanding, of the whole animal to give useful context.

Conversely, the danger of considering the whole thing, working on all of it, is that we move everything forward just an inch at a time. This is demoralising for those doing the work, and the stakeholders do not see any noticeable progress.

Organise the work so that you are able to show progress. Make sure people can understand the roadmap so that the approach does not look piecemeal.

Tackle the hardest things first, not the easiest. It is tempting to do the latter, to prioritise quick-wins or 'low-hanging fruit', and sometime this is necessary to get people onside, to make a tactical point, to boost morale by showing some progress. What it does not do is reduce the risk. By tackling the hardest things first we learn as early as possible about expected and unexpected difficulties. This early experience might show that we need an alteration in direction, emphasis or priority, and the earlier we make an alteration the easier it is to make.

Having said all of that, problems can arise late in the cycle too, and I strongly suggest that is it *never* too late to make an alteration. It is just that the later we do it, the more intensely we must scrutinise for impacts, and the more thoroughly we must communicate to protect the trust.

Referring back to the story at the beginning of this chapter, Alex was brave enough to say the unsayable and raise the 'do nothing' option. This resulted in stopping a programme of work, because the scope was huge and the beneficial outcomes were not well defined. We hope they moth-balled it in order to capture the value from the work done to date, ready for when they re-start later with a better focus on drivers and outcomes, and more manageable scale and structure.

Takeaways

- time, cost, function and quality are the generic dimensions - time is the most visible
- incremental, step and transformational changes have different management needs
- clarity in the required outcomes facilitates clarity of planning and action
- understanding the nature of the drivers helps to focus both strategy and tactics
- understanding the organisation shape & style informs both strategy and tactics
- it's what people *are* that makes or breaks a change – they don't usually alter very much
- ideally the change team is connected to, yet insulated from, the BAU operation
- the change team benefits from space to innovate, as well as rigour and discipline
- project mechanisms and methodologies are just tools to help us on our way
- a clear RACI matrix avoids confusion, duplication and all sorts of arguments
- always consider the 'no action' option, if only to tease out the consequences
- in a crisis it is best to think quickly and calmly, and act slowly – no panic, no knee-jerk
- eat the elephant (huge task) by seeing the whole thing but taking one bite at a time

6 Past and Future Pressures

As the five of them piled into the black cab out of the rain, it crossed David's mind that this could be a pressure-cooker ride for the next 20 minutes. Day 1 of a change manager's interim assignment was always interesting, and this one was a corker.

"I've got a feeling this could be a big one today, guys" said Hugo (newly arrived Sales Director, NewDiv) as they fought with folding seats and recalcitrant seatbelts. "Damn, watch your umbrella old chap" complained Julian (Operations Director of some 15 years standing) "and what do you mean by 'big one', this is only the first presentation." The others looked from old dog to new dog, wondering where this was going.

"We have to be very careful about making new commitments" continued Julian "because it takes time to understand the consequences, and we mustn't overstretch ourselves. Furthermore," he said warming to his theme "a lot of people need to be consulted, and we'll need a new multi-disciplinary committee to examine any new product proposal. This is how we've worked in the past, and it has served us well."

"Ah but Julian, that's not where we are now is it?" said Sandra (interim General Manager, NewDiv). "NewDiv has been given a mandate by the Board to find faster ways of working, because frankly our company has been overtaken by its competitors. We need to leapfrog forward, and that means developing new products and services with partners that are already into the new media, people who understand what's needed out there."

"Yeah," added Hugo "and there are plenty of small, hungry companies out there who respect the brand and market presence we have. When I told the XtoX company yesterday that we could deliver a service to them in 6-9 months they nearly bit my arm off. They are small of course, but it's a great sign."

The "whoa, hold on" from Sharon (product manager, assigned from OldDiv) and the "Great" from Sandra were drowned by a roar from Julian "You cannot have said that, I haven't even met XtoX yet, and we have no idea whether we can deliver in that timescale. What about growth projections, what about performance measurements, we have no idea whether this is sustainable."

David rubbed the mist from his window and gazed out at the traffic jam as he thought about the expectations from the old guard that this new venture would be a low-risk, small, careful step into new technology, and the conflict with the new team who just wanted to grab any opportunity to get into play as quickly as possible and manage their strategy from the hip. As the piggy in the middle he would have to do a lot of translating between the two, a lot of brokering between the different working paces.

Hugo interrupted David's musing by saying "Look, guys, all I need is Sharon here in the loop with me while we get some heads of agreement signed up - Sandra has delegated to us – we have to move quickly to get past the competition." Hugo had a small smile on his face which, thought David, whether through naivety or over-confidence was risking a major bust-up in this cramped and damp space.

"But you haven't got me in the loop, have you?" said Sharon in a manner that sounded both grumpy and resigned. "I don't know about yesterday's meeting."

"Ah, that's what you and I are meeting about later today" said Hugo, still with the irrepressible smile. Sharon looked grim and said nothing more, partly because it was clear that Julian was working up to another outburst.

"Now look," said Julian, struggling to keep his tone measured, "we have a long-established and highly valuable brand to protect and shareholder expectations to manage. We cannot go around making rash promises to fly-by-night companies. It simply won't do."

Hugo slid open the internal window to the driver and asked quietly "are we nearly there?" The driver's reply was inaudible, but Hugo's agitated body language suggested the answer was in the negative.

David felt he should start in on his peacemaker role, although he wasn't sure how much notice they would take of him on his first day ... this was far from an ideal starting point to build trust. As he breathed in before speaking, Julian made it clear he hadn't finished yet by wagging his finger in Sandra's direction before saying "This is a complex business, we have to tread carefully, we need to find the right opportunities and then run well-planned pilots to assess the cost/benefit, the likely demand, the support costs, and so on. You know this, it's why we brought you in."

"Yes, Julian, I understand where you're coming from" replied Sandra "but you also said we'd have some freedom to move quickly, to match the pace of the new, small companies in this space. To do this we have to take some risks. Otherwise we will be overtaken by events, and left with a dwindling old-style business."

"But we do need some controls on the commitments we make" chipped in Sharon quickly, "or we will disappoint everyone, from our management and shareholders to our new partners and their customers."

David saw his chance here to make a positive intervention. "I can help here, by working with Sandra and Sharon to manage the risk assessment around each opportunity, figure out the mitigations and how to monitor them. Then, with a market profile from Hugo and a costs profile from Sharon, the whole team will be able to compare the opportunities and decide which ones to prioritise into the programme you want me to manage."

"Hello, yes, this is Hugo" said Hugo into his mobile "I'm sorry we might be a few minutes late – we're stuck in a terrible traffic jam. Yes, fine ... I'm bringing our whole senior team to show you how committed our company is to this opportunity. Good, thanks, see you in a few minutes." The rain re-doubled in intensity as the cab moved forward a few feet.

This little story is a real mix of past and future pressures, of different assumptions and expectations. It shows the need for a very strong communication strategy just within this management team let alone to other stakeholders and communities. David's initial priority is to help each camp, old guard and new broom, to understand the other's position, and to rein in extreme attitudes and actions for the sake of the common good across all parties.

A change of any size is almost never without some history, predecessors, precedents ... and these are more likely to be negative than positive pressures from the past. It can be a bad IT experience, a marketing campaign flop, a strike, management politics, or even an external event such as supplier failure.

It is important to think outside the total scope of the change. We must understand what went before, in order to manage and adjust expectations. We must also seek to understand what will or may come after, in order to position and prioritise the components of this change to meet the identifiable future challenges.

Inherited expectations

Although history is always interesting, it is only really useful when it informs the future.

This might happen in a number of ways: reading the organisation's Lessons Learned database is the obvious example, assuming it exists; stakeholder perception is a less obvious but pretty important factor. In the story above there are historical habits and procedural baggage to overcome, which is not a simple task.

As we are frequently reminded by reputable journals and books, we continue to make the same mistakes (because we are human). We do so in ever more sophisticated ways and with larger consequences due to our ever increasing capabilities in technology and communication.

There are things we can do to mitigate the baggage that people arrive with into the change team, including agreeing ways of working together and accepting personal strengths and weaknesses and responses to pressure.

---

illustration: learn from history

In my career I have been involved in hundreds of projects, worked with thousands of people, and read & written tens of thousands of documents, presentations & internet communications. Not all of them were good, and it is from the less good that we learn most about how to improve. I have made plenty of mistakes. When I was young I used to scoff at stakeholder management theories, on the basis that the right solution is obvious and the stakeholders are senior and therefore experienced and smart so they will get it ... and I now know this is wrong, on a number of fronts. Sometimes they could not see it, or would not see it. Sometimes they could see it, although their interests were differently aligned from mine or the greater good. Sometimes they plain disagreed with me (and I suppose just occasionally they may have been right). Finally, not all stakeholders are senior managers.

I am sure that I'm still making mistakes, and I am still learning from them; it never stops.

---

team charter

A Team Charter can help to overcome past experiences and negative expectations – it must be worked up together by the team, physically signed by all, then I suggest you laminate copies for everyone to have at their desk. Just occasionally a physical reminder is a good thing. Here is a set of suggested items for a charter:

- email volume: use emails sensibly, only to relevant people, only when a phone-call is not sufficient – avoid lengthy email trails with large numbers of recipients – avoid multi-subject emails which then fragment into overlapping email trails – do not send documents as attachments, send links to where they are stored
- representation: all senior team members to have deputies who are fully briefed
- meetings: start on time, no waiting for laggards – formal meetings must have as much notice as possible, a clear agenda and required outcome, and appropriate briefing/preparation documents distributed 4 working days before – facilitation and minute-taking responsibilities agreed at the meeting start
- document review: if reviewers cannot manage the timescales of the agreed process cycle, they delegate the action or raise an issue immediately
- respect and trust expertise: listen to subject matter experts, challenge constructively if appropriate, and use their advice
- individual communication: endeavour to be honest, open, constructive, realistic – think about what the listener needs to hear – have "strong beliefs, loosely held" i.e. be able to explain and justify your position whilst being prepared to accept challenges, listen, discuss and modify
- fit-for-purpose: don't re-invent the wheel, don't prioritise things that are not broken – do prioritise gaps, do consider impacts in other areas
- positive response: when asked to comment on something, silence is not assent – always respond, if only to say 'ok' – all contributions should be presenting solutions rather than just describing the problem, and must not block progress
- focus on deliverables

personal dynamics

An assessment of how individuals respond in different situations can be done formally or informally, using various methodologies. It is unavoidably a sensitive area, and is better led or facilitated by a professional in the area of coaching and development.

There will undoubtedly be periods in the change when people are working under considerable pressure, and it is very helpful to have an understanding of how each individual responds to that. Some people adjust very little in how they manage themselves and interact with team members, management and stakeholders. Others undergo a radical alteration, which could be extrovert or introvert in nature.

This is not to say that we should seek to alter people's responses. The main benefit is to recognise the responses as indicative of pressure, and where it is counter-productive to do something about it. A further possible benefit is that through awareness of their response, the individual may be able to manage their responses to make them more positive.

---

illustration: working under pressure

I was once part of an assessment of working under pressure and managing conflict, using the Strength Deployment Inventory (SDI) methodology, and it clearly showed that some people altered their working style and approach quite considerably when coming under significant pressure, whilst others hardly altered at all. This is a useful thing to know, and we all kept the results chart to hand for reference during that particularly high-pressure programme. What we didn't do was to measure whether at the end of a period of working under pressure, people returned immediately or gradually to their former type, or indeed never returned.

Future challenges

Anticipating the future is invariably difficult in anything other than a small, simple organisation. Yet, as with many things, just because it is hard and error-prone does not mean we can avoid it. Even if many of the conclusions reached turn out to be wrong, there is value from the thinking and the awareness that future-gazing generates. Where we cannot have certainty, at least have awareness of the possibilities and the factors involved.

Gerald Ashley and Terry Lloyd in their book *Two Speed World* have much to say, both thought-provoking and entertaining, on the necessity and the difficulty of future-gazing to anticipate the need and impact of disruptive change. Their last chapter is a wide-ranging look at human history and the impending disasters or challenges that await us in our increasingly global society, whilst noting that human flexibility will probably allow us to find a way through.

predictions

In the introduction to *Future Shock*, Alvin Toffler wrote "No serious futurist deals in 'predictions'. These are left for television oracles and newspaper astrologers." He goes on to explain that although he speaks firmly throughout the book, in effect making predictions, every usage of "will" should be preceded by "probably" or "in my opinion". The main thrust of his argument, first written in 1970, is that the accelerating pace of social and technological change (probably?) will cause distress and disorientation (the current dictionary definition of 'future shock').

Toffler then says that it is more important to be imaginative and insightful than to be 100% right when thinking about what the future holds, and I think that is hugely important for anyone managing significant change. Just thinking about and discussing possible future scenarios, never mind which one is right, helps to inform the scope, strategy and planning.

There are many dangers for which we need to be alert, because our thinking processes are often not entirely logical. We are influenced by self-interest that presents in a number of ways, including self-image, respect of peers, standing in community, professional reputation. It is a rare person who cheerfully admits they are wrong about something, or even that they do not know something that perhaps they should know.

In *The Black Swan* Nassim Nicholas Taleb discusses very many interesting practical philosophies. One of these is Confirmation Bias where, once a person has made a choice, they accept only evidence that supports their decision and reject evidence that does not. When evidence that contradicts a prediction is found, a typical pundit will find an excuse to disregard it. Trust me, this occurs in change management as well: a future scenario (vision) is selected, and then defended against evidence showing it to be overly risky or even unattainable; a project overrun is denied, rationalised or hidden; a measurement is omitted, ignored or even adjusted (falsified).

timeframes

When looking for future challenges to factor in, to guard against, or simply to put on the 'watch list', it helps to have three different timeframes in mind.

There is the future that is within the timeframe of the change activity itself. This ought to be quite tightly predictable, and addressed within the analysis and planning of the change. If we find it is not, then this translates directly into risks for the change; we must ask some searching questions of ourselves, our sponsor, management and stakeholders.

Then there is the future immediately after the change has delivered, let's say the same duration as the change activity itself. Clearly this is at least the start of the payback period, and it is the start of proving the sustainability of the change. This period should be reasonably predictable, although other unconnected events or activities could easily have an effect on reaping the benefits. Ask yourself, from your experience and that of others both within and outside the organisation, about potential scenarios; analyse the scenario outcomes as you do for risks, in terms or likelihood and impact, and prioritise accordingly. The high scorers then deserve some intervention to mitigate their likelihood and/or impact, just before the change is delivered.

Finally there is the long-term future, the whole period over which the change is expected to have an effect, to be sustained, to survive. Here it is much more difficult to anticipate every possible impact, and it is quite likely we will not be there to see or handle them. The best we can do is to set up a list of potential impacts and consequences, with warning signs, and hand this on to the operational management.

finger on the pulse

Yours is not the only change going on in and around your organisation! As we have said many times, there is a lot of it about. So every thought, analysis, note and action regarding potential future impacts must be open to review at any time when new information becomes available.

The alert change manager has antennae that are constantly twitching, seeking alterations in the landscape, new data, anything that could be relevant to the work in hand. This could come from deeply formal documents such as annual reports, through to chance conversations in the kitchen.

Of course this cannot be allowed to pre-occupy us such that we under-perform on the main tasks. Nevertheless, we need to be constantly alert for anything new or unexpected – rather like the cat in the Digression on dogs and cats in Chapter 2.

KPIs to keep on track

KPIs or Key Performance Indicators are measures of progress which are more typically used to monitor incremental improvements in a BAU or operational context. An individual or a team might have an objective for the year, and linked with that are quarterly KPIs that indicate whether they are on target.

In a change project context, KPIs can be used along the same lines where there are activities with a long time-base and it is helpful to have quantitative feedback along the way.

digression: ultimate challenge

As I write this, a slow, remorseless tsunami of economic change continues to roll around the globe, first triggered by the seismic shock of the banking-led, first-world, multi-dip recession. The ultimate change management challenge is the world economy and the current model of capitalism. If we fail on this, we will not have the ability to handle the environmental changes along with ensuring there is breathable air, clean water and adequate food for everyone. We have to challenge the presumption that the only way out is economic growth for ever, because that simply is not practical, there are finite limitations.

In his book *Consumptionomics: Asia's role in reshaping capitalism and saving the planet*, Chandran Nair argues that economic policy must change. The alternative is a catastrophic outcome arising from relentless promotion of a consumption-led growth model in the world's most populous regions, at a time where resource constraints are a major issue.

Chandran Nair argues that the Western model of consumption-led economic growth cannot be replicated in Asia. This statement is not new, but Nair offers a new perspective from the Asian point of view. If the global community is serious about lessening the impact of global capitalism on the world's resources, then the role of the region with the largest populations on Earth must take centre stage.

He is arguing, controversially in this case, for benign authoritarianism. In fact this is the model in many successful organisations, and it works where incentives are sufficiently well-aligned from boardroom to coalface.

Manage complexity

A lot of the Change in organisations is complex – in other words there are many interdependent and interconnecting components needed to achieve the whole. Complexity introduces risk because it typically means that one person cannot have their head across all aspects of the change, which in turn means that multiple accountabilities are required, along with significant communication and governance overheads. Amongst all this is the opportunity for politics, confusion (wilful or not), duplication and dropped balls.

clean interfaces

A vital part of the change manager's role is to contain this complexity, in a way that reduces risk to the four key constraints: time, money, function, quality. One of the best ways to do this is entirely analogous to good software and systems design: clean interfaces between the components, meaning interfaces that are well-defined, covering all eventualities, and strongly managed. Then the activities either side of an interface can be safely delegated without jeopardising the integrity of the whole structure. This is the same principle as we discuss under **Management & team** in Chapter 5.

be strict on data

Data is the life blood of any organisation, whether it be enabling decisions, informing actions or measuring outcomes. The danger comes when there are very large amounts and the quality is unclear, for then it is difficult to extract reliable information from such data.

In anything other than the simplest activity, do ensure that a set of rules are agreed up front for data management, in other words how, and by whom, data is acquired, maintained and analysed.

These rules might include:

- how data is checked for errors when acquired
- who controls updates
- how a single master copy of data is made available to all relevant people
- who is allowed to analyse and interpret the data
- how the data is archived when no longer used

Rules like these significantly reduce the risk of wilful or accidental confusion, duplication of effort, and drawing mistaken inferences. If we agree them before any data is gathered, we avoid argument and re-work.

use any methodology

This is not a book about methodologies. It is appropriate though to discuss the benefits, and downsides, of using methodologies, for example PRINCE2 and Agile.

PRINCE2 is a highly sophisticated project management methodology & toolkit, able to handle large and complex projects. It epitomises the waterfall approach where planning, analysis, development, testing and delivery are all done in separate, sequential stages. It assumes the ability to apply a very deterministic approach, even to formulating the change project. How does it deal with poor estimating? Stealing of resources? Impractical time-boxing? It doesn't.

This is my mapping of the processes (across) against the documents (down) in the <u>full</u> usage of PRINCE2. You don't need to be able to read the text to see that it is complex.

Key: Output, Update, Approve, Input, X=part of Quality Plan, B=part of Brief	SU						IP						CS									MP			SB						CP			PL							DP				
	1	2	3	4	5	6	1	2	3	4	5	6	1	2	3	4	5	6	7	8	9	1	2	3	1	2	3	4	5	6	1	2	3	1	2	3	4	5	6	7	1	2	3	4	5
MANDATE	I	I		I																																									
SU																																													
Exec/PM Job Desc	O																																												
PM Team structure		O										I													U																I				
PM Team Job Descs		O	O				U			U		I																													I				
BRIEF				O	I	I	I	I	I			I																						I							A				
BUSINESS CASE				B					U			I				I	I			I							U	I	I			I	I										I		
ACCEPTANCE CRITERIA				B			X																																						
CUST QUALITY EXPECTN				B																																									
RISK LOG				O	I	U		U	U	U		I	U			U	I	I	U	I		U			U	U	U	U	I	I		I	I			I			U		I		I		
DAILY LOG				O																													I												
APPROACH					O	I	I	I	I			I														U								I							I				
IP STAGE PLAN						O																																		<<	A				
IP																																													
PROJECT QUALITY PLAN							O	I		I	U	I													I	U							I	I	I										
CONFIG MGT PLAN							X																								I														
QUALITY LOG							O						U	I			I	I			I	U	U	I	U				I	U			I												
PROJECT PLAN								O	U	U	I	I				I	I			I					I	U	I	I		I			U							<<		A	I		
PROJECT CONTROLS+TOL										O		I																																	
COMMUNICATION PLAN										O		I						I											U		I													I	I
ISSUE LOG											O		U	U	U	U	I	I	U	U					I	U	U	U	I	I	I	I	I												
LESSONS LEARNED LOG											O																		U				I												
PID												O								I					I					I	I		I	I								A	I		I
CS																																													
WORK PACKAGE													O								A	I	U	U																					
PRODUCT STATUS ACCNT														O																I	I														
PROJECT ISSUE (NEW)															I	U																												O	
OFF SPECIFICATION															I	O																													
REQUEST FOR CHANGE															I	O																													
HIGHLIGHT REPORT																		O																										I	
EXCEPTION REPORT																				O										I														I	
MP																																													
TEAM PLAN														I								O	U																	<<					
CHECKPOINT REPORTS														I				I					O																						
SB																																													
CURRENT STAGE PLAN													U	U		I	I	I	I	I					I	I		I	I	I													O		
NEXT STAGE PLAN																									O	I			I											<<		A	A		
END STAGE REPORT																													O													I	I		
EXCEPTION PLAN													U			I										I		I	I	O										<<			A		
CP																																													
FOLLOW-ON ACTION REC																																O													A
POST-PROJ REVIEW PLN																																O													A
LESSONS LEARNED REP																																	O												A
END PROJECT REPORT																																	O												A
PL																																													
PLAN DESIGN																																		O	I										
PRODUCT BREAKDOWN																																			O		I		I						
PRODUCT DESCRIPTIONS													I																						O	I	I		I						
CONFIG ITEM RECORDS													U	U			I		U	U	U								U		I		I		O		I		I						
PRODUCT CHECKLIST													U	U			I	I	I																O		I		I	U					
PRODUCT FLOW DIAGRM																																			O	I	I		I						
ACTIVITY LIST																																				O	I		I						
ACTIVITY DEPENDENCIES																																				O	I	I	I						
ACTIVITY ESTIMATES																																					O	I	I						
SCHEDULE																																						O	I						
THE PLAN																																								^					

For projects that are small in size and/or simple in scope, the full application of the methodology is far too large an overhead, and creates the risk that the methodology becomes an end in itself instead of simply a tool in achieving the required project outcome.

This is true of any methodology, and I counsel you to proceed with caution and hold the enthusiasts and evangelists at arm's length. It is best to choose one methodology that is closest to what we need, or with which most of the people involved are familiar, and then treat it as a toolbox. Select from it what is appropriate and useful, and use that subset consistently. The benefit comes from having a common framework of procedural rules and language that everyone understands, but only as long as it does not become a ball & chain on everyone's ankles.

What of the Agile method, then, the latest religion (as of 2016)? There is an irony in that PRINCE2 and Agile were built up in parallel through the 1990s, yet people perceive waterfall as 'old' and agile as 'new'. They were very differing responses by very different groups of people, to the same challenge of delivering complex technology solutions. Agile was created as a more responsive, less tightly structured way of managing software development, and has now spread to many more areas including change management. There is an informative eBook by Melanie Franklin called *Creating an Agile Environment for Effective Project Management* which explains the Agile concept and talks with examples about how she introduces Agile approaches into companies.

To my mind Agile's strength is in putting analysts, builders and testers together to work in short time-boxes whilst closely connected with the customer. This avoids two weaknesses of the waterfall: that an error in the planning or analysis does not show up until months (or years) later during testing or deployment; and that the customer's priorities or requirements change unseen during the project, causing a mismatch at the end. Agile is probably not the answer to all problems, and of course has weaknesses of its own: it can appear to allow fudging of unknowns and lack of clarity and commitment. The flip side of flexibility, in timing, function and delivery, is uncertainty ... and by now you know my view that uncertainty is a very bad thing and must always be eliminated. There is more on this in Chapter 7.

Agile comes into its own in two circumstances: first where the requirement is not clear and some experimentation is needed – although a proof-of-concept or pilot project is another name for how to proceed; the second is where the change can be delivered in flexible, useful chunks that build up towards the complete requirement. A good example for the latter is a business process change. A poor example is a new office block – the foundations and the central lift shaft are not useful in themselves, yet they had better be right before continuing.

My preference is to be agile within a fit-for-purpose waterfall framework for whatever change is being managed. Some things just have to happen in the right order, yet there is considerable benefit in having all the players close-coupled with frequent reviews and opportunities to re-assess priorities. In a sense my whole book espouses an Agile mentality: listen carefully; speak well; be responsive; manage flexibility.

A lean approach to waterfall

I coined the term 'Lean PRINCE2' to mean a pragmatic usage of the core features in the methodology, to gain the benefit without over-investing the time and effort. I call my own version of this MECHANO (Managing Effective Change in Any Organisation) which is summarised in the diagram below.

There are three different degrees or levels of methodology that can be applied to projects (no doubt there could be more, but why complicate matters):

- Minimum: simple, single-phase project
  – core features only of the methodology i.e. 'Lean'
- Medium: complex, single-phase project
  – core features plus further controls esp. at Initiation
- Maximum: complex, multi-phase project
  – fuller usage of the methodology

The decision on which category a project fits into is a judgement call, and the change manager with the project executive makes this at the start. In general, though, the more Lean the better.

The essential thing to retain in a reduced or lean methodology is the correct control & decision points. The essential principles are:

- stage & gate
- business case review
- governance
- sign-off
- report by exception

It is essential to exert some discipline in controlling what stage we are in at any one time – that is not to say we cannot zip backwards & forwards, be agile or even chaotic (as a tactic, not a strategy), as long as everyone is clear on, and agreed on, where we are and why we are there.

my MECHANO framework

The five Stages in the following diagram are I think self-describing, from Start-up through to Close. Between them are Gates through which the project must pass before it can proceed from one Stage to the next.

Life-Cycle of a Change

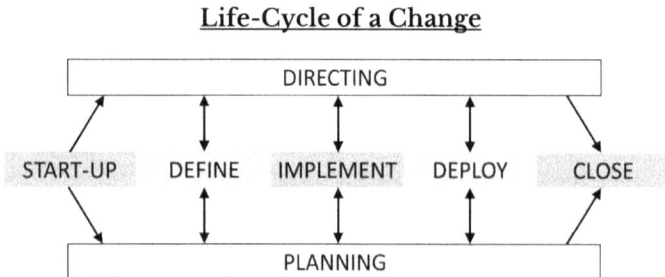

These Gates consist of reviews by relevant Stakeholders of the status of the project as represented by presentations, interviews, documents, evidence, and tests as appropriate. The reviewers should not be afraid to push back and ask for re-work or better information; the Gate must be a real, meaningful barrier.

Note that the Directing and the Planning activities are continuous across all Stages.

In a small or simple change, the structure can be made even more Lean. As a bare minimum, every project must have a Start, Middle & End, and the beginning of each is an essential control point:

Start = Start-up & Define – all the thinking
Middle = Implement & Deploy – all the doing
End = Close – all the wrapping up

Sustainability

Sustainable change does not mean sustaining the process of change, it means sustaining the benefits of the change long after the change has been made. We should always talk about sustainable beneficial change. Not least because there is plenty of change around that is not particularly beneficial or where the benefits simply do not last. Of course beneficial can be defined in many ways and for many different profiles or priorities of stakeholders.

There is little point in making a change if that change does not 'stick'. As discussed in Future Challenges earlier, sometimes a more far-sighted forecasting is required, verging on clairvoyance. (A Chief Clairvoyance Officer would be an excellent resource ... if dependable.)

This forecasting might be as simple as analysing all the dependencies in the operation, or it might require sophisticated scenario modelling that looks at the organisation in the context of the whole world around it. The important thing is not just to ask ourselves "what could go wrong in making this change?", but also to ask "what could weaken or undo it after it's done, and how can we reduce that risk?"

Here is an example of structuring change to be sustainable in the face of evolving circumstances. An air travel organisation was moving into a new building and consequently changing its business processes from top to toe. The inter-connectedness of all the processes was so familiar to those at the coal-face that it was not discussed, meaning that a small variation in a planned change in one area would ripple through the whole process structure. The approach taken was two-fold: first to prioritise the definition of the connections between discrete business processes, rather than the processes themselves – if the connections are sustained then the whole structure is sustained; second to set up rolling reviews to capture and share lessons learned and sign-off on incremental improvements both during and after the changes.

Measurement before and after

A change that is not planned, communicated, managed and has no defined, measurable benefits will be chaotic and will most likely fail. As we discuss in Chapter 3, without measurement we cannot know quantitatively and reliably the extent to which we have succeeded.

It is simple madness not to check that a change has generated the expected beneficial (or otherwise, but definitely expected) outcomes and impacts.

So we must measure after the change has been deployed, using the same approach as the measurement before so that we can compare like with like and assess the genuine differences. It is true that in some cases the measurement might be of an absolute, which needs no comparative measure. The majority of changes are more in the way of improving something, and for that we need to know the measurements of that something before the change, so we can compare with afterwards and see the degree of improvement.

An example of an absolute change is a new warehouse building where nothing existed before; we could say that the warehouse functioning according to plan is an absolute, with no relevant 'before' measure. Yet even here I contend there are comparative measurements that are of interest – it is likely the warehouse has more modern design, equipment and processes, and part of the rationale may be based on it being more efficient ... so we want to know how much more efficient and for that we need 'before' measurement from other warehouses.

To measure and reap the benefits from a change there must be a period of 'no change' or steady state both before it and following it. Without this the whole success of the change is subject to confusion, obfuscation and distrust. The settling time for a change varies, before we can make a meaningful measurement; each should be planned, especially in a linked series of changes.

In the planning stage for a change, then, it is necessary to work out what we are going to measure and how we are going to do that, for both before and after. The first priority is to identify measures that will show the success of the change. In addition I strongly recommend that we identify things that are *not* supposed to alter and figure out how to measure them before and after too; this helps to alert us to unintended consequences.

By the way, there is nothing to say we cannot measure *during* the change. There may well be things that are changed gradually or in small steps, and a regular measurement is part of assessing progress. We need to be careful about opening this up to the BAU operation though, as it can generate 'change fatigue'.

When looking at a measurement number always ask yourself whether this is a *significant* number. Significance arises from the context and the consequences. A large number is not always important or impressive or even meaningful, no matter how impressive it may sound. Conversely a small number that is a doubling of a previous small number could be extremely significant.

In some cases the impacts are quickly and readily seen. In other cases it may require some ingenuity to reveal the true impacts, or it may take some considerable time for them to appear.

Except in the most enlightened of organisations, it is highly likely that those managing the change will be off doing other work by the time the 'measurement after' is practical. It is therefore incumbent upon those change managers to pass on to their operational counterparts the information, background, data and techniques that will facilitate a successful measurement.

Takeaways

- history is only really useful when it informs the future
- people arrive into the change team with baggage from their previous experiences
- a team charter created by the team provides a framework for working together
- it is helpful to know beforehand how each person responds to pressure
- although anticipating the future is difficult and error-prone, we must not avoid it
- beware of Confirmation Bias that blindly defends/ignores problems in a chosen vision
- like the cat, we must be constantly alert for anything new or unexpected
- managing complexity, and protecting people from it, is a key skill for change managers
- methods & processes must be as 'lean' as possible whilst still being fit-for-purpose
- there is little point in making a change if that change does not 'stick' or sustain
- we need to measure before the change as well as after, to assess the success

7

Blockers and Distractions

Janet ticked people off on the Programme Review attendee list as they straggled into the room. She thought, not for the first time, that as programme director she ought to have a project admin person handling the meeting mechanics – pity she'd finally lost the budget battle on that one. One of today's major topics was a risk that had turned into an issue while she was fighting for the project admin budget.

"OK, it's 11 o'clock so let's get started" said Janet standing up, "please close the door. There's a few people still to come, and they will have to catch up." She was gradually training the team that the meeting start time was not the time you stroll down the corridor to the coffee machine and have a natter on the way back.

"The programme review this month is internal. This means it's the whole team of project managers, analysts and subject matter experts. There are no programme board or other senior managers here. We are going to focus on the risks and issues registers and I want you to be open and honest and constructive. There is no need to be defensive, assign blame, or cover things up. With 20 of us here we are going to need some discipline so let's make sure we have one person speaking at a time, and please listen and think about what is being said. I am chairing, and I won't allow long discussions – we have 2 hours and we need some concrete outputs." "Oh," Janet added "and each risk and issue owner is responsible for taking notes and updating the register entry, and John here has volunteered after some arm-twisting to take meeting notes so I can see nothing gets missed."

A hand shot up at the far end of the room. "Please miss, when are the biscuits coming?" Janet smiled "thank you Ragbir, I know I can rely on you to defuse any tension later."

The meeting had only progressed to the third risk when someone said "but surely this is an issue, not a risk, it's in the wrong register". "Well," said Janet "are you absolutely certain that this will happen, or has already happened? If so you're right, and if not then it's avoidable or at least reducible, and stays as a risk." The meeting then descended into a debate on uncertainty, how it is much worse than known problems, and quite forgetting the one person speaking rule, until Janet dragged them back. "Ok, everyone, let's listen to Chandra, she's the owner on this one."

"It's definitely an issue, because the Union vote happened last week, it's well documented" stated Chandra now that she could make her voice heard "but I don't know how to fix it, I need some suggestions please." It is surprising how quiet a room of 20 people can be when challenged. "We need to schedule a meeting to deal with that" said an elder member of the squad "probably early next week." "No, no, no" said Janet "we already have everyone in the room who can contribute to this, that's the whole point, and we won't know any more next week – we need to discuss it and decide now." "But we haven't got all the information" said the elder. "No, and we never will have," replied Janet "we have to make the best decision now on the information available, or it will delay other work. If we don't contain this issue it will contaminate the whole programme"

It wasn't long after the meeting had grappled with making a decision, when the next challenge emerged. "The last risk just says 'External constraints' - Magnus, we need more specifics, can you explain?" Magnus leaned forward conspiratorially and said "there's the possibility that we might be taken over next year, and this could invalidate all our work here." A low murmuring around the room. Janet knew that Magnus was very earnest and would take a put-down badly, so she softened the blow "Ok, it's good to think very broadly when identifying risks, so that we can then refine the set we work on. Our programme is due to deliver by mid-year, with measurable benefits by the year-end. So we're going to keep this risk, but as 'no action' because there's nothing we can do about it and it doesn't impact our delivery, unless we're very late."

"It's all very well making these decisions" said Agnieszka "but I'm worried we are wasting our time here, because the Board won't sign off on them if they haven't been involved, and the Union isn't formally represented here either, and the Ops Director has never supported this programme, he's just waiting for us to trip up." "Those are all valid concerns" said Janet quickly before the ever-threatening cloud of gloom settled into the room. "However if we treated them as reasons to stop progress we'd never get anywhere. We have a clear governance structure, signed-off budget and

> deliverables, and a good stakeholder management plan; let me handle the politics while the team gets the work done." The room brightened visibly as they discussed and agreed actions for the remaining issues.

We can see in this story an organisation that is habituated to putting things off, welcoming distractions, finding reasons for inaction. Janet has an uphill battle on her hands to get her programme team working with a more positive, assertive, can-do mindset.

At any and all points in the life-cycle of a change, things crop up that threaten to either get in the way or to siphon off effort and focus. These range from conscious, destructive manipulations through to innocent, incidental events. Everyone involved in change must be alert to this.

It is all too easy to slip into the mindset of "I cannot make progress because ...", or "before I can make progress I must deal with ...". Instead, the mindset we need to create and maintain is "I can continue progress by doing ...". We can achieve this by resolving uncertainties, keeping focus on the outcomes, understanding the people and politics, and containing the effects of unexpected events.

My strong advice is to jump on blockers and distractions early; do not let them fester, and definitely do not let them breed.

Problems v. uncertainty

Problems we can deal with – it is uncertainty that kills us. Problems always have solutions, whether palatable or not, and decisions can be made even if the data is poor.

Uncertainty blocks decision-making, wastes time, and saps morale. As you are probably realising, I do not like uncertainty. If a change manager has a single mission in life, it should be to seek out and resolve uncertainties. (Of course she has many missions, this is just one of the most important.)

problem management

There is a healthy debate about the management of messy problems, in the general sense of having some idea of what is wrong and no idea of the solution. Many think there is a danger in breaking down a large problem into smaller parts, some of which are easily solvable puzzles, because we will lose sight of the overall problem, lose the context of what we are doing. Ashley & Lloyd in Chapter 3 of *Two Speed World* refer to Russell Ackoff's definition of messes, problems and puzzles, and they quote Michael Pidd's caution about breaking up messes into smaller pieces that are treated as puzzles.

I disagree. It is highly advantageous, especially when faced with a huge problem (cf Eat the Elephant at the end of Chapter 5) to break it down into manageable chunks. The way to do this without losing sight of the whole picture, or wandering off into solving a different problem, is to define and then manage the interfaces between our chunks (see **Manage complexity** earlier in this chapter). We also need someone (typically a programme manager) to retain the overall view of connections and dependencies between the chunks.

When implementing something that has complex multiple deliveries over a tight time period it can be worth constructing a matrix of functional areas against delivery dates. This is easier to look at than a conventional project timeline plan; it is not how we get there, it is what happens to the BAU operation and when.

Keep logs of everything: worklist, donelist, issues, risks, dependencies, decisions, assumptions, change requests. Having all this information at our finger-tips keeps us sane and avoids going back over old ground, or wasting time searching through emails and meeting minutes, when problems arise. It also facilitates swift response to queries from Sponsor or Stakeholders, which sustains trust.

There is another matrix that is very helpful when managing a lot of projects with complex interdependencies. List all the projects across the top, and again down the side. Now for each project, working down the side, you can go across the row and indicate which other projects have a dependency on it. Better still you can enter R for Red, A for Amber or G for Green to indicate the current status of that dependency. Print it out every time you update it, for instance at weekly programme & project reviews, and stick it on the wall. It gives us a broad feeling for how things are, and clearly shows any hotspots of difficulty.

assumptions about uncertainty

There is a lot more potential for uncertainty around than you might think.

For example, you might say to me "it will be ready by Thursday". That seems pretty certain, right? Wrong. This is uncertainty through being imprecise. Does it mean first thing on Thursday, so I can schedule a dependent action during Thursday, or does it mean last thing on Thursday so I have to wait until Friday. Come to that, if say it is Tuesday now, which Thursday are you talking about? I have had this happen, where in two days' time you say to me "oh, well, I meant *next* Thursday ... obviously". It was not obvious to me. These situations are countered by not accepting imprecise statements, by asking qualifying questions. Some people hate it, and call us pedantic, to which we gently point out the consequences of making the wrong assumption. Others may learn from it and be more precise in future.

There are two causes of uncertainty that require mini-projects: there is the Uncertain Sponsor - they don't know quite what they want, but they will recognise it when they see it; and there is the uncertainty because we have not done this thing before, we don't know anyone who has, and there is no reasonable way of accurately estimating or predicting the outcome. We talked about this earlier when discussing the need for pilot or proof-of-concept actions. Don't build a sophisticated castle of a change management plan with a foundation of loose sand. Identify what you can do to resolve or significantly reduce the uncertainty, then do the pre-work that ensures a foundation of concrete.

Let's say we need to make a decision, and the factors affecting it are too uncertain for us to have much confidence in that decision – at least we are short on facts to back it up. A helpful technique here is to acknowledge that the decision will to some extent be based on instinct, hunch or informed guesswork. Then make the decision, privately, without acting upon it – instead sleep on it. This is a 'trial' decision. In the next day, or two, we see how comfortable we feel about the trial decision. We might even test it out against some others, as long as they understand the rules of the game. You may be surprised at how much more objective and rational you feel about assessing a trial decision, compared to assessing the uncertain factors that bear upon it. Sometimes the day after making it we can see that it is obviously not the best decision – by looking at it from a different position.

Finally if we still have some uncertainties left then put them on the risk register, and monitor and re-assess them on a regular basis. The review cycle may be anywhere between daily and monthly depending on how quick- or slow-moving the circumstances are.

Focus on the end state

In Chapter 3 we talk about Starting at the End, Focus on outcomes, and Working back. In Chapter 4 we cover Strategies and Tactics to keep us on the rails. Here we talk about maintaining all those things, keeping our head whilst all around us are losing theirs ... and helping them too.

manage our head

When everything is going smoothly according to plan, then life is easy for the change team. No, actually, life is never easy. At times like this the alert change manager and her team are constantly on the lookout for blockers, distractions, problems and risks as yet unseen. Periodically she is also checking on the end state, that it is still viable, still the required outcome, and has not been affected by external events. Certainly this is all positive activity, and so whilst never easy it is enjoyable.

The going gets really tough, of course, when multiple things are going wrong and a sense of crisis is building in the team. This is the time for re-doubled focus on that end state and everything needed to maintain the progress towards it. Keep your head up, keep a strong sense of the vision, don't be indecisive, do make decisions in the big picture context. Recognise your strengths and weaknesses, be open to getting help in the weaker areas, just don't delegate or dilute your authority. Don't get dragged down into the dirty detail because you need to keep your head clear and focused ahead; have trusted people summarise the detail for you. In the end we, and the project, are judged by what is done, not by what is promised.

rescue other heads

Others in the project team may be badly affected when things go wrong or problems arise. They may be less experienced and less capable in handling bad news and mounting pressure. Having led by example as per above, we need to literally take them to one side, sit them down, and talk through how to contain the bad stuff and put it in the perspective of all the existing positives.

---

illustration: false start

Here is a practical example of recovering from doing the wrong things for the right reasons. A division of a company had been criticised in an audit, with a list of 12 required action areas. They rushed off to tackle all of them at once, because they had promised resolutions within a single tight deadline. Yet many of the areas were interdependent, and requiring resources from the normal operation ... so duplication, confusion & frustration reigned. The recovery action was to stop everything, look at the big picture and which actions best deliver against that, map out the sequence of actions according to dependencies and resourcing, construct a realistic timeline, and re-negotiate a sequence of deadlines with the auditors.

---

change control

We digress into this in Chapter 5; the business of controlling alterations within the project itself.

Even with the very best effort at the outset to create a strategy and a plan that covers all possible eventualities, unforeseen bad stuff still happens. Or risks do materialise into issues. There are times when the project does need to be altered in some way, to defend the delivery of the required outcomes. In extremis, the outcomes might be altered themselves; reduced perhaps, or phased, as long as they remain within the acceptable range of outcomes originally defined.

Apparently minor alterations within a project can have an insidious effect if not very carefully controlled. A series of minor adjustments might be entirely justifiable one by one as having no discernible effect on the efficacy of the project, yet the cumulative effect of them together may be considerable.

To combat this, every project no matter how small must have a change control process. This process requires any change to be researched, discussed and documented, before submission to a change control committee for approval (or otherwise). The biggest job of that committee is to look for unintended consequences.

beware the Sawtooth

It is not uncommon for a project to have trouble 'breaking through the benefit surface' to deliver something of value to the organisation. When it gets close to delivering there is some problem which causes a retreat, then when it is close again another reason for retreating is found, and so on. This is what I call the sawtooth below the surface, and is illustrated in the diagram. Until the project breaks through to deliver benefit, it is simply a liability.

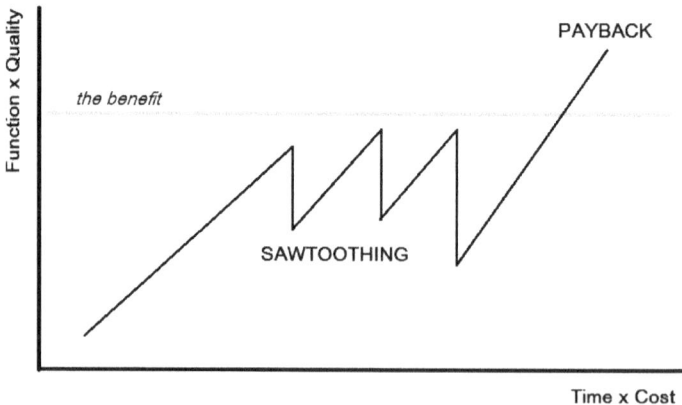

The reasons for this sawtoothing are usually one of three types: the project was badly formulated, and final tests or quality checks keep failing; the team lacks the courage to put their collective heads above the wall or necks on the line; or there are external forces at play which don't want the project to succeed.

You can look elsewhere in this book if you need help on the remedies for the first and last of these reasons. The second reason, lacking courage, is an interesting one and I have witnessed it a number of times. It may be rooted in lack of confidence, for good or bad reasons, or previous bad experiences, or simply inexperience.

The way to push through the benefit surface to the payback zone is, you've guessed it, to help everyone to focus on the project end state, and to ensure that all stakeholders have a positive and constructive attitude.

People

We make strenuous efforts to ensure that we utilise fit-for-purpose technology systems and business processes, yet how often do we really ensure that the staff are fit-for-purpose? Not just in terms of knowledge, skills and experience – they also need to have the appropriate style, temperament and character for the various roles.

People's attitudes stemming from their previous experience can be a huge blocker to change. This may be habituation to comfort or defensiveness from conflict. It may be seated in a single recent event or in years of bitter experience.

Talk is cheap, as they say, and indeed talk alone does not achieve a lot. Yet talk is essential, as is listening. Sometimes attitudes can soften simply from having the opportunity to be heard. A sympathetic ear, who can then gently put the negatives into perspective and can remind about the positives, can work wonders.

Meetings can become huge distractions, or if properly managed they can be effective for communication, team-building, enabling, even decision-making. More on this in the next chapter.

keeping it positive

There will be dips and frustrations in any change project. If before that happens we have built a positive high, then the dip may only take us back to where we started, from which we can bounce back, rather than taking us into a hole from which it requires a much bigger effort to climb back up. The gradient and distance may well be the same, but the psychology is hugely different. It is not enough for there to be no attitude issues; we must strive for a very positive attitude at all times, as a defence against the occasional, unavoidable dip.

There are times when firm words have to be spoken, when people have to be reminded of their position and responsibilities and the way in which they should conduct themselves. Have your fights in private. In public find the positives and be supportive.

I like to ban the following phrases: "pretty much", "almost there", "more or less", with a charity 'swear-box' if the culture allows it. The reason is that these are subjective assessments and get-out phrases, often used to hide a lack of progress or an uncertainty of status. We have got to get it out in the open, because finding out what we don't know is very, very useful.

Furthermore, in discussions we cannot allow any of the following because they invalidate the discussion's conclusions: "I think it has/will be agreed"; "we don't know yet"; "this needs to be decided later".

grief and stress

Elisabeth Kübler-Ross originally defined the 5 stages of grief on death and dying. David McWilliams in *Follow The Money* picked up on them in relation to economic failure. It is instructive to think of them in relation to people's poor reactions to a proposed change:

1. denial
2. anger
3. bargaining
4. depression
5. acceptance

Thinking about whether and where people might be on this cycle helps in seeing things from their point of view, aligning yourself, and therefore making a more effective connection when trying to engage them and bring them to a positive understanding. It is not a guaranteed formula; there's nothing that is. All these things are tools to be selected at appropriate times.

Change can cause pressure which can lead to stress. Denis Sartain & Maria Katsarou in their book *Under Pressure* make the point of individual responsibility very forcefully. Despite the UK Court of Appeal guidelines stating that the employer should be proactive in looking after the mental health of employees, for instance by providing access to a confidential advice service, the employer is not held responsible unless they have been informed of some particular problem or vulnerability. It is the individual's responsibility. The same holds true in a change team. Nevertheless, it is a foolish employer or change manager who does not watch out for warning signs.

People under stress often act and respond very differently to how they normally operate. They may try to hide, they may become very defensive, or indeed they may go into overdrive. Whilst not exactly discussing 'good stress' and 'bad stress', which has become a popular topic in the 21st century, Sartain & Katsarou do discuss the inevitability of pressure and how certain amounts and types of pressure are a good thing and usually necessary for progress. They also point out that the more conscientious a person is, the more likely they are to become stressed.

activity illusion

Activity is all too easily an illusion of productivity. The mantra needs to be "it's not the work that counts, it's the outcomes".

Ian Price puts it nicely in referring to his book *The Activity Illusion*: "everyone I worked with was frantically busy and yet so little was being achieved; this appeared to me to be the case the more senior the manager. I worked with people who were "too busy" to perform the basic functions of leadership - too busy to have team meetings, too busy to delegate, too busy to give feedback." These people were hiding from their responsibilities.

I am not suggesting that we should be quantitatively measuring everyone's productivity – outside repetitive tasks, and certainly in change projects, this is hard to do in a meaningful and repeatable way, and may not even be practical. Of course, measuring the work effort *will* be useful for informing future estimates of effort required. It just doesn't help much in delivering the goods this time around. The better approach is one of educating and encouraging everyone to think in terms of, and take pride in, outputs rather than inputs. As ever, it is up to the change manager to be alert to the workaholic or perfectionist who despite all that effort is delivering late ... or delivering on time whilst ruining their health and happiness.

shared resources

There is often the challenge of the people resource not being fully committed to the change work. They may have responsibilities in other projects, or worse still they may have operational responsibilities that always trump the project work. Ideally we separate them and have dedicated resources, but that is not always practical in smaller organisations or where a particular expertise is needed in multiple projects. So very careful management is required with an openness to the problems that arise – the bottom line is that operational priorities often blow even the most pessimistic of project timelines – this can be mitigated by knowing and managing the operational processes very tightly.

politics

The definition of this term that I have in mind here is "activities aimed at gaining power in an organisation". Clearly this is more than choosing the timing and style of communications to suit the foibles and preferences of our audience, which is only an extension of 'speaking for the listener'. It is more than saying or doing things differently according to location to accommodate different cultures, as this is good practice. It is more even than face-saving exercises during difficulties, which can be quite acceptable tactics. We need to dodge turf wars, and know when to be quiet to avoid drawing fire.

I'm sorry about the combative language. That's what this kind of politics uses, and we need to be aware of it. The one thing we must never, ever do is get drawn into it and feed the fire.

If the politics is coming from junior levels then we need to deal with it; not necessarily ourselves as it may be passed to HR. If it is coming from senior levels then it's unlikely to be manageable, and dodging and deflection is the best we can do. If it is coming from our peers, this is the biggest challenge, and we have to stand our ground and think always what is best for the project. If it is sapping time and energy, then the issue must be escalated to the Sponsor in the first instance. This kind of issue is better discussed with and aided by an individual rather than a committee.

---

digression: IT in perspective

There is no such thing as an IT project. I'll say it again ... there's <u>no</u> such thing as an IT project. Just as the furniture in the boardroom does not make the decisions, so IT does not run the organisation. All projects are **'business'** projects, although many are influenced by, facilitated by, or reliant upon IT. Even the project with 100% IT content, such as upgrading an organisation's wide-area network, is not done for IT's sake, it is done to deliver benefits to the organisation. The measurement of success must be focused on those benefits, not driven by the technical performance.

It is fair to say that in the 21st century most organisations could not function as well as they do without IT, and the sudden loss of IT services makes most organisations stagger to some degree, and kills a few stone-dead in very short order. IT is a vital support function, just like Finance, Legal, HR, and Procurement, but whose loss is felt more quickly.

Do not be confused by the example of the organisation whose business is selling IT products or services. In this case there is IT that <u>is</u> the business, and there is IT <u>within</u> the business that is the supporting function. All projects are still business projects.

Containment

Unexpected stuff happens, and because it is unexpected it usually appears to need urgent attention. Everybody rushes over here to fight this fire, rushes over there to dam that flood. A poorly planned and badly managed project spends a lot of its time 'fire-fighting', with everybody busy and the project going nowhere.

Urgency is often relative or subjective. It is ok to push back against new demands, to ask what are the consequences of us ignoring this (for a while at least), or deflecting it into a new direction.

external resilience

The purpose of this component in the change management toolbox is to proactively protect the efficiency and effectiveness of the change work by shielding it from external factors.

This is probably the hardest area of all, looking outside our area of control, competence, even knowledge. The 'unknown unknowns' are out there, waiting to get us. We have to go looking for some things we suspect, to make them visible, and we have to scenario-plan where, within reasonable time constraints, no scenario is too crazy. A small investment in external expertise, people who have trodden the same path, may pay huge dividends here alongside our own 'what-if' thinking.

Again, this also provides another sanity check on the robustness of the outcome delivered into the real world. If we cannot see any dangers, then we haven't looked hard enough. Too many dangers, and we might want to reconsider the viability of the change.

parking lot

This is a reactive technique, similar to that used in exploratory or brainstorming meetings.

If something comes up that must be handled, but this is the wrong time, then log it in the 'parking lot'. As in a meeting, this assures people (and reminds you) that it is not ignored, it is visible, and it will be handled at the appropriate time.

Just make sure that the parking lot list is visible to everyone, and do review it regularly

what to drop

It sometimes comes to the point where something has to give in order to maintain the overall project outcomes. Some reduction in activity or delivery has to be accepted. We have to slide down the range of acceptable outcomes.

The question then is, what do we stop doing? Answering this is a whole lot harder than it sounds. We are well into the project, we have done a good job of team-building and communicating, there is intellectual and emotional commitment to all components of the project. Now we are going to drop a couple of components; people will feel hurt, morale will sag.

The reverse problem, and a common one, is that the resources (people, money, time) are reduced yet senior management still expects all the same outcomes. Clearly, people just have to work harder, right? Maybe occasionally there is slack that can be taken up; in general though, this is not so easy.

We need to refer to the four-way tension early in Chapter 5. My view is that time, in other words delivery dates, is the last thing we allow to change. Decreasing function or quality or increasing cost are all up for grabs, although the latter is rarely a real option. Varying the quality is rather difficult to generalise on; it is very dependent on the nature of the deliverables.

To make the optimal choices in reducing the functionality, we need a list of the effort for each item compared to the eventual benefit. The prudent change manager, especially if anticipating a scenario such as this, already has such a list to hand. It does not need to be, and realistically cannot be, precise. The point is to be able to make a meaningful comparison. I know, the items are rarely so independent that a simple choice can be made from such a list. Nevertheless even in complex real-world situations, this approach helps and furthermore it gives us some kind of audit trail as and when our decisions are reviewed.

Takeaways

- problems we can deal with – it is uncertainty that kills us
- keep logs of everything; information at our fingertips avoids delays and duplication
- make charts, logs, statuses etc easily visible online and on the wall – it keeps the focus
- in an uncertain start-up, do a mini-project first to clear the uncertainty
- when multiple things are going wrong, re-double the focus on the end state
- anticipate team members experiencing stress, be proactive in providing support
- beware the 'sawtooth' project that consumes huge resources and delivers nothing
- beware the senior managers who are 'too busy' to provide even basic leadership
- strive for a strongly positive mindset at all times, as a bulwark against problems
- contain the effect of unexpected events

8 How to Make People Happy

"Hello, hello, can you hear me?" "Who else is on?" "This is Nicky in Milano." "Hi, Rupesh here in Bangalore." Steve in Austin, Texas sighed and wondered when the teleconference was going to get going. The chair must have signed in or they wouldn't be able to hear each other, so where was this recently-hired global programme manager? Steve left his mute button on while listening to the chatter with half an ear, thinking about the teleconference briefing papers sent a week ago; they had explained how we are 'one company' now and would have a single joined-up 'global learning service'. It sounded like economies through fewer staff to him, despite the apparent intentions to increase the 'learning delivery'.

"Hello everyone, this is George Langster, I'm the Global Programme Manager in London chairing this call, and the UK Training Manager, Linda, is on the phone from her office in Bristol. Welcome everyone. Now, the team on this call don't know each other terribly well, and it's not easy on the phone. So, just to hear each other's voices could each of you say your name and job title as I run through the city and country list, thanks. So let's start with Vienna, Austria please?" With the introductions across 15 cities in 12 countries over, George continued "Thanks everyone. Now I'd like to talk to you about the global plans, the responses we've had so far, and then open it up for you to ask any questions on any aspect of this." Steve thought it was unlikely anyone would ask the real burning questions on an open forum to someone they didn't know. He'd already talked to his local line manager about whether redundancies were likely, because he knew him and could read the body language. It didn't look good.

George had been talking about the shift to online learning to provide more flexibility as Steve was typing an email to his manager group about the next set of classroom courses, when he caught the word 'redundancies'. He wound up the volume in time to hear George say "I can confirm there are no redundancies in any of the training groups; your skills and experience are all needed. Yes, there will be less admin overall on a single system, however we will rotate responsibility for the admin around the major centres, and you will now have more time to work on new learning content. The first challenge to all of you is to participate in the configuration design of the new learning system which is multi-media and encompasses informal as well as formal learning."

Steve released his mute button "Steve here, in Austin, can I ask a question?" "Hi Steve, sure, go ahead" "This new system will take a long time, and we have real problems today – is everything going to freeze now for a year?" "Great question, Steve, I know about your issues" replied George "and no, we won't freeze – the company recognises we have to keep up the small wins while preparing the huge leap forward." "Ok, thanks" said Steve, smiling for the first time that day.

Then a question from the young man in China "how will we operate as a global team when the time differences are so great?" "Yes that's a good question" jumped in Rupesh "and the training content is different too in different locations." "Ok, thanks" said George "the main ways we'll handle those logistics are an online open forum, and a rolling zone teleconference – more on that later, and I do appreciate that today it's very early for some and horribly late for others. What I'd like the team to focus on now is what we share, what we have in common" Steve added 'consistent assessment' into the melee of positive suggestions that followed. He had always thought it unfair that different levels of achievement around the world had been awarded the same certificate.

As George wound up the teleconference with talk of regional calls and shared design document reviews, Steve reflected that this global stuff didn't sound so bad after all if it meant he'd have help in delivering to his area, and would have more time to improve the content and reach more people.

Happiness is a state of mind. The factors are many, and the priorities to achieve it differ wildly across different people. That said, there are obvious, common approaches and attitudes that will at least maximise the opportunity for happiness.

In my simple analysis:

Happiness = $\dfrac{\text{achievements x respect}}{\text{expectations x frustrations}}$

For context, a *GfK NOP poll* for the BBC showed that among seven broad factors influencing happiness, 'fulfilment at work' was a top-3 factor for 19%. This apparently leaves 81% of our colleagues with work as only a minor contributor to their overall happiness. In which case why am I devoting a chapter to the subject? There is a narrow and a wide answer to this.

The narrow answer is that typically when people are at work, the work context is a much larger part of how they feel, compared to when they are at home. (As an aside, I wonder where they were when completed that BBC poll?) Furthermore it is quite possible for people to be happy at work whilst unhappy outside it, as well as the reverse. Therefore 'work happiness' is a bigger factor when working, and is definitely something worth understanding and influencing.

The wide answer is the other side of the coin, in that unhappiness outside work, depending on the factors involved, can affect a person's work performance. Now whilst we may not be able to influence the causes, it is worth at least being aware of it.

What I am really addressing in this chapter are the things that oil the wheels, that help people to feel good about what they are doing. In many ways this is the opposite of the previous chapter on blockers and distractions.

Steve in the story above is clearly focused on providing a great service to his customers within the organisation – that, and still having a job, is what makes him happy. His unhappiness at the start of the teleconference meeting comes from rumour and his own scepticism. George the programme manager handles this well by focusing on a practical communication strategy, on positive actions for everyone, and by having an awareness of individual situations such as Steve's. George has done his homework and it shows.

In Chapter 2 we talk about Maslow's 'hierarchy of needs'. In an organisation we can assume that the first, physiological, layer is a given (although some may claim that work canteens can be injurious to life). Above that layer it is all to play for.

Talk in their language

All areas of activity have their own language or vocabulary. This is useful as a short-cut, to speed up communication, and also to ensure common understanding. On the downside, it can be used wilfully to exclude those not familiar with it.

The change project is no exception – there is a whole new lexicon involved here for many people. We cover **speaking for the listener** at some length in Chapter 4 – this is the same point here.

Talk to them in their own language, explain things in terms with which they are comfortable. Then provide translations into project speak, or the new dialect of business speak, where necessary or where it is helpful. The more we can help them bridge the language gap, the more they feel they are inside the project rather than outside it. Be careful though to extend their comfort zone, don't drag them right out of it.

Don't let your communications turn into marketing that creates false belonging, false expectations. Give accurate information, don't sell wishes and desires.

Effective meetings

Properly used, meetings are an essential part of the framework for communication, inclusion, and action. Yet they are one of the biggest breeding grounds of unhappiness, as well as loss of time and energy. So often they are called for the wrong reasons, with too many people or the wrong people, and at the wrong time. These are common refrains. In many organisations there is an enormous, inefficient consumption of people's time in meetings.

wrong content

Another typical difficulty is when there is some 'churning' going on, where important issues are discussed in multiple meetings, yet no progress or decision is made. People derive a degree of misplaced comfort from just talking about the issue, as though that alone improves the status. It may well make them feel better, and that is a small win that can be worth having, but progress is always what is needed.

Then there are the meetings where a lot of experienced & bright people are discussing key issues in mid-air. That should be productive, you might think? Only if they have a strong facilitator to keep it on track, and a well-informed scribe to make sense of and record the conclusions and actions.

Yet another 'great' meeting is where an enormous amount of work has been done to document what we are supposed to be doing, and yet the documents are ignored and everything seems to be up for grabs again. We must let those documents underpin everything, and if a document is wrong then it must be corrected through rigorous change control and with a transparency that ensures everyone knows what has changed and why.

---

illustration: stuck looking back

I inherited a regular review meeting structure on a large programme in a FTSE-100 company. The 'way we do things' had a huge amount of history, or to put it more negatively, 'baggage'. The first item on the agenda was always 'Minutes of the previous meeting', (which were often not available until shortly before or even at the meeting), and the second item was 'Matters arising'. This meant that the first half of the meeting was spent discussing what was previously discussed, going over old ground, making grammatical corrections, and then picking up on subjects to take forward as it suited the most vocal or forceful of the attendees. It was a huge waste of time and effort, it confused people, and was frankly a playground for politics. It also meant that people with no axe to grind had a habit of turning up randomly late, in an attempt to avoid this unproductive part of the meeting.

I fixed this by doing two simple things. Firstly I ensured the Minutes were circulated within 24 hours, with a note that any factual errors must be raised with me immediately. Secondly I moved the 'previous meeting' item to the end of the agenda.

right approaches

Be clear about the objective of a meeting. Is it to generate ideas, or to share information, or to assign actions, or to make or endorse decisions? All of these things benefit from the interaction of a group of the right people in a room. It won't work if the attendees have different views on the expected results from the meeting.

The people necessary for the meeting are required to attend. Others who are interested parties can receive the documented meeting output. Meetings need defined objectives & strong management. All attendees must do their relevant preparation.

The right briefing and preparation will ensure that any meeting only needs a light touch of kindly discipline to keep it on track.

When holding small meetings of, say, 2 to 4 people, be clear about the formality, or lack of it. We can discuss awkward issues in a small group that would be impractical or a poor use of time with a large group. Just make sure the attendees know whether they are on or off the record.

formal meetings - chair

Invite only those who we need to participate or who will benefit from participation – make it clear who is required, and who if any is optional.

Be clear about the objectives and agenda. Make briefing documents available if appropriate at least 24 hours before.

Start on time. Manage the agenda and attendees to ensure the agenda is covered.

Finish 5 minutes before the end time.

Ensure that the outputs are documented and available to all participants within 24 hours – ensure people are aware where they have actions from the meeting.

formal meetings - attendees

If you are a required attendee, make every effort to attend. If unable to attend, give the Chair the earliest notice and provide written or verbal input to the Chair. If only able to attend part, arriving late or leaving early, tell the Chair before it starts.

Arrive on time, prepared to start immediately, having read any documents available and prepared your inputs and questions.

Switch mobiles off or to silent. Only accept calls relating to urgent operational issues, and step out of the room to accept the call.

Keep all discussion concise and to the point. Think about what others need to hear as well as what you want to say.

brainstorm sessions

A Brainstorm by definition is an exploratory or investigative discussion looking for ideas on a particular subject area/opportunity/challenge, among people from different backgrounds, without limits (within reason).

Nevertheless, as with any meeting, it needs management/facilitation so that it is productive and that people feel it is time well spent and it still needs a beginning, a middle and an end.

Beginning – stated by the chair/facilitator

Decide who is going to take notes and how – if possible it is best to write on the walls (flip-chart sheets and sticky notes) so everyone can see what is captured.

Ensure people know each other's backgrounds and areas of expertise – it may be appropriate to go round the table giving each person 1 minute (maximum!) to summarise this.

State the focus of the discussion e.g. "we're here to talk about bag-drop in the terminal".

State the scope, what is in and what is out e.g. "we're not talking about history, except where it teaches us something for the future – we're looking for an ideal solution, then we'll try to find a route from where we are today – don't feel constrained at this stage, any ideas are welcome".

State the desired outcome e.g. "in this session we're just looking to capture ideas and grade them in terms of practicality" or "we need to build on the ideas and figure out a roadmap to achieve them"

Middle – chair/facilitator manages 'in the background'

It really depends on the participants as to whether the discussion needs stimulus by a contentious statement or two (it is always worth having a couple prepared), or whether some people need curtailing ("please could you just summarise your point so we can capture it") whilst others need bringing out ("you may not have specific knowledge of this, but what is your feeling on ...").

We may need to bring the discussion to a summary, by referring to the captured information or reminding the group about the scope, and then let it flow again, in order to retain the focus.

End – stated by the chair/facilitator

Summarise the outcome and get agreement from the meeting on that.

Thank everyone for their participation.

Commit to sharing the written-up outcome (if appropriate).

Invite further input by telephone or email to you.

State what happens next, and how they can/will be involved (as appropriate).

Openness & reliability

In the opening chapter of *Under Pressure*, Sartain & Katsarou discuss "what's happening in the world of work"; they point to the increasing danger of cognitive dissonance due to the much larger range and volume of information available in this communication age in which we work and live. Cognitive dissonance is the term coined by psychologist Leon Festinger in 1954 to describe "the feeling of psychological discomfort produced by the combined presence of two thoughts that do not follow from one another". Put more bluntly, if you believe your organisation is in trouble yet the senior management say everything's fine, you will probably experience a discomfort called stress; your job could be on the line. Sartain & Katsarou conclude by stating "Honest information, therefore, is the key. People are owed that honesty, however unpalatable, so they can make decisions and feel they have some control. When people don't have the information or answers – or [they are given] inadequate or inaccurate information – they often seek to address the cognitive dissonance they feel by making it up, sometimes with harmful consequences to themselves and the organisation." In other words the rumour mill starts, and that is never a good thing.

Again this is an issue of trust. Can we trust the organisation in which we are working to be honest with us? Can we maintain the trust of staff reporting to us by acting honestly ourselves?

communicating

There is plenty on this in Chapter 4, in terms of mechanisms. I am adding a few points here about what people like to hear.

Don't deal with too many topics at once, and keep the message simple. Make it obvious whether this is information only, or whether this is a call for action of some kind. Always, always, remind people of the communication back-channels available and encourage them to provide input.

You can keep in your own mind my 'Three-C' approach to ensure the message hits home:

- Clarity
- Conciseness
- Consistency

This last point is often where things slip up. For instance if we are periodically updating people who are Consulted and Informed in the RACI matrix of roles, we must assume their thinking has not moved on since our last such communication. For us, a hundred small things may have progressed and so we have a very different context. If we write the next message from our own context it will not make sense to those people, it will appear inconsistent from the last missive. This is another example of speaking for the listener, in this case linking forward from what they last heard.

understanding

To establish and maintain a stress-free understanding across all stakeholders I can recommend my 'Three-D' approach to the main subjects for information updates:

- Drivers
- Deliverables
- Dates

These are the three external dependencies, the why, what and when, that matter to everyone. Other parameters can be flexed, such as the who, how and where, without altering the big picture. If you can keep the Three-D consistent, and most especially the Dates as I have mentioned before, then people will trust the project, and trust makes people happy.

responsibility

It is important that the responsibility given to an individual is aligned with their incentives, and that they are given the authority to match the responsibility.

In some cases it may work the other way around, in that the delegation of responsibility to an individual has a positive effect on his incentive. Certainly, the right kind of responsibility promotes a better sense of belonging and reduces the 'us and them' syndrome.

There is also the possibility to assign collective responsibility to a group of people, and let them sort out how it is managed between them. We do need to be pretty sure of our trust in them and our understanding of their incentives, and how we monitor or measure their progress. Otherwise we will end up micro-managing the situation which then disempowers the group and makes a mockery of the delegation.

documentation

Never dismiss any requirement ideas completely, simply put them on an appropriate priority list, the last of which is 'not in scope for this change'. This ties into inclusion & belonging by not dismissing any input, other than the obviously daft, as unusable.

Use the programme log to document not only risks and issues but also assumptions, change requests, decisions, quality checks, and ad-hoc actions. Make it open for all to read.

no (bad) surprises

In general, surprises are not a good thing. They knock people off balance.

The ideal change project is of course fully planned with plenty of contingency, and perfectly executed to deliver exactly what was required and expected. Ok, it is fair to say that is rarely the case. Stuff happens. The successful change project handles the stuff that happens and still keeps the overall benefits on track.

It is inevitable that occasionally there is an unexpected bad news event. Don't try to hide it, don't try to bury it under other messages. Deal with it openly in a positive context. Don't ever talk about just the problem, always talk about the problem and the solution, or range of solutions, or at least the approach to figuring out the solution.

---

digression: transferable skills

Many change interims like myself have transferable skills between industries, although clients are often resistant to the idea. As a Change & Programme Manager, the skills & experience I have are around strategy, structure, organisation, planning, communication, reporting and measurement. The principles, and a lot of the practice, are the same wherever we are, because there are fundamental rules of business and people are people.

Nevertheless clients often insist that such a role must also be a subject-matter-expert. In my view this can be positively dangerous, as the interim manager risks getting sucked into and distracted by the detailed design work and problem solving, whilst losing sight and control of strategy, stakeholders and deliverables. Whereas someone highly experienced yet fresh to the industry or functional area can deliberately ask the 'dumb questions' that challenge preconceptions or assumptions and shake out risky or unprofitable corporate habits.

Quick wins

I do talk a lot about the big picture, and keeping events and information in context. On the other hand, a quick win is a time-honoured approach to pleasing staff, management and stakeholders alike. It is especially important when needing to build or re-build trust within the organisation or to boost morale.

There are broadly two approaches to generating a quick win. The first is to select some small thing that is easy to do, with little or no preparation, and no dependency on the rest of the project; the 'low-hanging fruit' approach which delivers part of the overall outcome very early. The second is to make a very rough cut of a significant proportion of the change and let all stakeholders see that and give input, before going back and re-working everything; the 'iterative' approach that may repeat this cycle 2 or 3 times, and gives early insights into what the outcome will look like. Some would call this Agile working.

The best approach, if indeed either are workable, depends on the nature and size of the change, the time and cost pressures, and the views of the stakeholders.

There are risks of course with going after a quick win or two in either approach, in that it may drag the overall change off course, or it may send the wrong message to some groups of stakeholders. So the communication and management of expectations around any quick win must be very carefully handled.

Ethical dimension

It helps a lot if people feel good about the organisation, and about the change they are going through. 'Feel good' can mean many things to many people, and can be a minor factor for some and a huge factor for others.

Those working in not-for-profit and charity sectors generally are more inclined to be there because they believe in and support the cause. Those in commercial organisations generally are more likely to be there because the work interests them and the career attracts them, or they simply need the money. Even in the latter case, more people are paying attention in recent years to the effect the organisation has on the world around it, the Corporate and Social Responsibility (CSR) angle.

We can apply the CSR thinking even to a change within an organisation, at least to establish that it does not reduce the organisation-level CSR commitment and track record.

This is an area that is open to scepticism, even cynicism. All aspirations, messages and commitments must be very carefully worded, and of course they must be real and not just lip-service.

Inclusion & belonging

Do we adapt people to perfect systems, or adapt systems to imperfect people? I am sure you can make the right call.

We talk about winning hearts & minds in Chapter 2, which gets us part of the way there – at that point there is an acceptance of the 'rightness' of the change, though not necessarily the sense of being part of it which is the really powerful factor. This belonging aspect of having happy, productive people has cropped up all over the book. The holy grail in managing any change is that ALL those involved or affected are positively engaged in the change.

seeking engagement

In *Prosperity Without Growth*, Tim Jackson starts by examining what we mean by, what we expect from, the term 'prosperity'. He uses the term to mean the wellbeing or happiness of an individual on the widest scale, rather than the narrow meaning of financial status. I suggest that in the work context, this broader prosperity is partly derived from a sense of belonging, of feeling part of it, of feeling included. Furthermore, people who have a feeling that they belong to a change, or indeed that the change belongs to them, are open to becoming positively engaged, if not so already.

Belonging comes from an understanding, both of the change rationales and the context for the individual. Delivering this to all participants requires a clear, believable strategy, well-defined outcomes, and great communication through multiple channels. Obvious stuff, yet often left aside in the flurry of planning, resourcing, financing and re-planning.

Many years ago while working for Dow Jones I was in New York as part of a 'new business' team. The company organised some performance coaching for us, and I clearly recall one sporting metaphor from amongst the mumbo jumbo and high-fiving. We were continually asked "are you in the stands or are you on the pitch?", meaning are we observing and criticising what is happening, or are we participating in some way – are we dissociated or associated? As with most metaphors, it doesn't do to examine it too closely or it starts to break down; we can argue that someone in the stands who is shouting encouragement is indeed positively engaged, and someone on the pitch might for whatever reason be a saboteur. It is really a question of thinking about and monitoring attitudes and expectations.

So look for individuals who are not constructively engaged and observe them, research them, and talk with them to find out why they don't feel they belong. Perhaps despite all our excellent communication, it passed them by – a localised blip. Or perhaps it points up a systemic failing in the change programme's communication strategy. Or perhaps they have too narrow a role and need their monotonous, repetitive job to be broadened and varied so that they become more interested.

importance of words

In all communications make sure you use words that actively include your target audience, and ensure there is nothing contradictory or confusing for any other recipients. Assume that everything will be read by everyone even if you do operate restricted circulations.

It is much more powerful to say "this might be helpful to you" than to say "this is the most wonderful, unique, life-altering thing ever" – people who cold call me with offers of services should take note. It is also usually more effective to start a conversation with "It would helpful if you would ..." rather than "I need you to ..." or "Why have you not ...".

Barack Obama's ever-present 2008 presidential campaign slogan was "Change we can believe in". If he had bothered to ask me, I would have suggested that "Change we can be a part of" is far more effective in because it is inclusive. I'll ignore the fact that both phrases end in prepositions. Still, it was a good rallying cry and the campaign maximized their message by creating a clear goal and funnelling all their energy towards garnering support to achieve it. Obama focused on three key words: Hope, Change, Action. Interestingly this is a focus not on outcomes but on the desire to alter the status quo, which is the usual approach of politicians (it seems to me).

In change projects within organisations it is important, unlike political campaigns, to avoid rubbishing the status quo or the changes that have gone before. Learn from them in a constructive way, of course, but don't disrespect them. Many of your team may have worked on them.

what I do counts

It is a healthy mindset within an organisation for everyone to understand how their job contributes to the outputs of the organisation, the products or services that are delivered – in other words the value of their job. It is pretty obvious in sales & marketing, slightly less so in R&D, but what about the facilities staff? It's a fact that the appearance and ergonomics of a building affect the morale of the staff, and morale is one of those magnifiers for productivity – a slight dip can cause a much bigger fall. Everyone does count.

President Kennedy asked a cleaner at NASA what his job was, and he answered "I'm helping to put a man on the moon". Although no doubt apocryphal, it is a nice illustration, a rather extreme one, of associating a job directly to the mission within a huge organisation.

Every role in an organisation should be describable in a maximum of three steps away from that organisation's deliverables. Everyone in the organisation should be able to say how they support the mission, vision and values – how many steps away from direct action. We can tease this out by asking "if I don't do my job, what happens, what sequence of consequences arise?" If this understanding is in place, it can smooth the path of organising change; we only have to help people understand the 'delta' – the change in their role and contribution in relation to the overall well-understood framework. If it is not in place, and people are unclear about the contribution of their job anyway, then the announcement of a significant change can create hiding in cupboards and wailing in toilets – scenes of distress and anger.

So ensure there is a framework in place that allows people to see clearly how their job contributes to the organisation's success ... before starting to talk about the changes. Then we can see how each person *belongs* in the overall framework of the change.

Takeaways

- happiness in work and outside work can be linked, and it helps to be aware of this
- if people feel good about what they and their organisation are doing, life is smoother
- talk to people in their own language and context, translate to project/business speak
- communicate accurate information, be honest, don't slip into selling wishes and desires
- meetings need thorough preparation, strong management, comprehensive follow-up
- three-C communication: clarity, conciseness, consistency
- three-D information: drivers, deliverables, dates
- deal with bad news openly in a positive context, discuss the problem and the solution
- quick wins can generate happiness, just be careful about negative consequences
- people need to see clearly how their role contributes to the organisation's success
- the holy grail of change is for everyone involved or affected to be positively engaged

9 Final Thoughts

None, I repeat none, of the contents of this book constitute hard and fast rules. I simply encourage you to use what you find relevant, to try out some aspects that are new to you, and store away the other interesting stuff for the future.

The strategy of my approach has been to lay out, in a loosely structured way, a lot of observations, illustrations, suggestions and advice for you to browse through and select. Alongside that strategy I allow myself a hope (see below), that you take away something useful having been stimulated and entertained on the way.

Before you go, here are a few last topics and a final summary as a reminder. Or if you are a contrarian who is reading from the back, then here are a few apparently random topics and a summary to whet your appetite.

Hope is not a strategy

"I hope xxx will happen" or "I hope you can do yyy" are phrases all too commonly used by people at all levels in an organisation, and they are very dangerous. The speaker goes away feeling they have politely asked for something to happen, yet the listener feels that it's ok if the thing does not happen because it is desirable but not required let alone essential. A serious mismatch in expectation.

Of course, if both parties are mere observers of the thing that may or may not happen, then this is just passive commentary which is acceptable though hardly useful. Normally however one or both parties have some desire, need or responsibility for the thing happening, in which case a more constructive and assertive statement is required, something like "What do we need to do to ensure that xxx will happen?"

Although this might appear to be a small or overly-analytical point, my contention is that laziness in language comes from laziness in thinking and leads to laziness in doing. So when someone says "I hope …", reply with a smile "hope is not a strategy" and then discuss what they really need and expect and with what priority and urgency.

A Top Ten "Do & Don't"

I was privileged to run a 9-month intensive programme of work, responding to a commercial crisis, in which the senior management were very self-aware and open to learning lessons from experience. They were not, it has to be said, very experienced in running a large programme of multiple projects in a structured and disciplined manner. As part of the programme closure, after successful delivery, we held some meetings with everyone involved, to capture experience and knowledge which should benefit future work. The following is one of the outputs of those closure meetings, a list that was much debated, refined, edited and tuned before it was signed off and distributed:

- Do have programme and/or project managers in place at the outset, with Terms of Reference and a clear governance and decision-making structure
- Do define the deliverables, do a gap analysis, plan by working back from the end, include contingency time, accept that learning on the way may cause a re-plan, and manage expectations

- <u>Don't</u> accept accountability for delivering until adequate resources have been committed
- <u>Do</u> define roles & responsibilities for everyone in the team, identify their support & training needs, define deputies for key roles, use & trust experts from the start
- <u>Do</u> track and document progress & issues fully, with a clear escalation process and effective decision-making
- <u>Don't</u> leave assumptions invisible, or sacrifice quality for time, or lose discipline, no matter how fast you are moving
- <u>Don't</u> use quick fixes, or hope problems will solve themselves, or work in isolation
- <u>Don't</u> react by jumping to solutions before thinking through the problem
- <u>Do</u> make communications a priority inside & outside the programme/project, incentivise & reward the team, promote & develop in-house resources
- <u>Do</u> consider external support/workshop during the programme to improve communication, understanding and team-work

Handling partial success

We won't always succeed completely, in whatever role we play in a change within our organisation. Even if we apply intelligently all the relevant material in this book, along with appropriate management and governance methodologies, plus best practice financial controls, supplier management and so on ... there are still a hundred things that can go wrong and are out of our control.

A mindset of partial success is of course far more helpful than a mindset of partial failure. Without wishing to be accused of being 'clever with words', it is also helpful to talk about what was unsuccessful rather than what failed. Failure is generally perceived as a rather black and white thing, whereas the reality is more likely to be on a sliding scale. If a change project delivers 40% of its intended benefits, is that a failed project? No, it is a mixture of successful and unsuccessful outcomes.

One of the most common constraints against us successfully using the relevant contents of this book is unenlightened management, whether senior or junior to our position. There may be little we can do about that directly, in which case use Gandhi's exhortation to "be the change you wish to see". Don't be distracted or dragged down to their level, instead let's be firm in how we wish to do things and be prepared to justify ourselves if challenged. You could of course lend them this book (and if you are lucky and I am lucky, then they will buy their own copy).

The negativity that may surround the unsuccessful outcomes can be mitigated, sometimes even banished, by an honest and constructive examination of what went wrong and how to minimise or avoid repetitions. The Lessons Learned review exercise can be a cathartic process for everyone involved, as long as it is run in a positive and inclusive manner.

To sum it all up …

Here is the takeaway of takeaways:

- the holy grail of change is for everyone involved or affected to be positively engaged
- problems we can deal with – it is uncertainty that kills us
- there is little point in making a change if that change does not 'stick' or sustain
- clarity in the required outcomes facilitates clarity of planning and action
- strategy protects the change from internal & external pressures, blockers & distractions
- predictability generates trust, and trust removes barriers
- always talk about the positives because people buy into success
- the understanding and usage of incentives and trust are the cornerstones of change
- and finally … expect the best and plan for the worst

It is ok to find a lot of these things hard to do, and to get things wrong occasionally. It really is. It is important to try, and through trying we get better. It is ok to fail sometimes as long as we are honest about it and learn from the experience. It is important to learn from our failures or partial successes, and apply that learning as soon as possible. By doing and learning, we grow.

Above all it is important to listen, to really listen; not only to what people are saying but also to why they are saying it, how they are saying it, and what they are not saying. This helps us to understand their incentives and their level of trust, and therefore the actions we must take to improve their engagement, their contribution, their productivity, and their happiness.

Epilogue

This book is not 'right' because there simply isn't a single right way to achieve successful & sustainable change – I trust that much is obvious. I am very interested to hear your thoughts, suggestions and experiences, on this book and on the wider subject of change management – please do contact me through my website at www.nicvine.com.

I can talk about the central points of this book as a workshop, conference or after-dinner speech, with the style and informality of the delivery suited to the occasion. If you think that your organisation might benefit from a discussion and shared understanding of this book's content, then please get in touch through my publisher website at www.trenchantbooks.com.

As to what the future holds for the discipline of change management ... *reaches for crystal ball* ... I see through the mists a complex future. Our abilities to understand, manage and modify incentives will improve very slowly – much more slowly than our abilities to wreak intended and unintended change in our societies, economies and environment. The consequence is that selecting, defining, managing, measuring and sustaining beneficial change will be more and more challenging.

The next twenty years are going to be highly frustrating, inspirational, risky and rewarding times to be involved in managing change, and whatever your participation I wish you the best of times.

Thirty years from now will have seen the generational changes, and it is even harder to call the outcomes. It is possible our civilisation could be starting to collapse – it has happened to others before us. Alternatively our unprecedented technological capabilities could allow us to manipulate our path away from disaster, towards a more stable and egalitarian group of societies that are capable of melding their individual histories with the common global good for the future. I choose that alternative.

Terminology

Here are my definitions of the generic terms I use:

benefit, impact, outcome, output - these are terms with overlapping meanings, and others may use them in slightly differing contexts, so let's be clear here:

- a benefit is something specific that is required or expected, is delivered and measured, and is usually ongoing or sustained
- an impact is an observed or experienced effect on the status quo, sometimes outside the scope of the change or even outside the organisation, often transitory
- an outcome is a material result usually described in broad terms more detailed than the vision and less detailed than the delivered benefits
- an output is the result of a specific action, such as a meeting or a re-plan

business as usual (BAU) - the existing status quo, the regular, established, operational activities of an organisation.

change - the broadest term for what is happening when we transition individuals, teams, and organisations from a current state to a required future state, by altering, adding or removing some components in the existing status quo.

organisation - the group of people (supposedly) working together towards a common commercial or social goal, wherein a change of some kind is to be executed. The organisation can be of any size and type: company; partnership; co-operative; government; institution; not-for-profit; charity; voluntary. It could be a global corporation involving many thousands of people, or a voluntary team of 3 people, or anything in between.

project - the generic term for the group of people, money and activities to create and deliver a change, and may encompass multiple projects of varying sizes and duration, grouped into **programmes** which themselves may be grouped into **portfolios**.

senior management - the high-level decision-makers in an organisation, typically at board level or one level below and certainly with significant budget responsibilities and authority.

six sigma - a management philosophy originally developed by Motorola that emphasises collecting data and analysing results to a fine degree as a way to reduce defects and variability in products and services.

staff - anyone working within the structure of the organisation, including both **employed** who are permanent or fixed-period with taxes administered by the organisation, and **contract** who are engaged for specific skills and usually on a project basis and administer their own taxes – the latter is an umbrella term for **temp, freelance, contractor, interim** and **consultant**, each of which have their own focus for deployment.

References

Ashley, Gerald & Terry Lloyd, *Two Speed World* (Harriman House, 2010)

Asimov, Isaac, *The End Of Eternity* (Voyager Books, 2000)

BBC, *GfK NOP poll*
(http://news.bbc.co.uk/nol/shared/bsp/hi/pdfs/29_03_06_happiness
_gfkpoll.pdf, accessed April 2016)

Blastland, Michael & Andrew Dilnot, *The Tiger That Isn't* (Profile Books, 2008)

Cable, Vince, *The Storm* (Atlantic Books, 2009)

Cameron, Esther & Mike Green, *Making Sense of Change Management* (Kogan Page 2nd ed. 2009)

Feynman, Richard P & Ralph Leighton, *"Surely You're Joking, Mr Feynman!"* (Vintage, 1992)

Fowler, Alan & Dennis Lock, *Accelerating Business and IT Change: Transforming Project Delivery* (Gower Publishing, 2006)

Franklin, Melanie, *Creating an Agile Environment for Effective Project Management* (Melanie Franklin, 2014)

Gilb, Tom, *Quantifying the Un-quantifiable* (https://www.gilb.com/blog/quantify-the-un-quantifiable-tom-gilb-at-tedxtrondheim, accessed April 2016)

Hart-Davis, Adam (editor), *History* (Dorling Kindersley, 2007)

Impact Executives, *Survey on Change* Impact Journal Issue 29 pp 14-17, Issue 31 pp 12-15 (http://www.impactexecutives.com/journals, accessed April 2016)

Jackson, Tim, *Prosperity Without Growth* (Earthscan, 2011)

Jennings, Charles, *The 70:20:10 Institute* (http://702010institute.com, accessed April 2016)

Kahane, Adam, *Transformative Scenario Planning: Working Together to Change the Future* (Berrett Koehler, 2012)

Kay, John, *Obliquity* (Profile Books, 2010)

Knight, Roger, *The Pursuit of VICTORY* (Penguin Books, 2006)

Levitt, Steven D. & Stephen J. Dubner, *Superfreakonomics* (Penguin Books, 2010)

Lewis, Michael, *The Big Short* (Penguin Books, 2011)

Maslow, Abraham, *A Theory of Human Motivation* (Psychological Review, 50(4), 370–96, 1943)

McWilliams, David, *Follow The Money* (Gill and Macmillan, 2009)

Midgley, Mary, *The Solitary Self: Darwin and the Selfish Gene* (Acumen, 2010)

Morieux, Yves of Boston Consulting Group, *Smart Rules: Six Ways to Get People to Solve Problems Without You* ((Harvard Business Review, September 2011 and online at https://www.bcgperspectives.com/content/articles/organization_desi gn_engagement_culture_hbr_smart_rules_six_ways_get_people_so lve_problems_without_you, accessed April 2016)

Munger, Charlie, *The Psychology of Human Misjudgement* (www.rbcpa.com/mungerspeech_june_95.pdf, accessed April 2016)

Obama, Barack, *The Audacity of Hope* (Canongate Books, 2008)

Paul, Richard and Linda Elder, *The Miniature Guide to Critical Thinking Concepts and Tools* (Foundation for Critical Thinking Press, 2008)

Pink, Daniel, *Drive: The Surprising Truth About What Motivates Us* (Canongate Books, 2011)

Pink, Daniel, *RSA talk on Drive* (http://www.thersa.org/events/rsaanimate/animate/rsa-animate-drive, accessed April 2016)

Powell, David, *Tony Benn – A Political Life* (Continuum, 2001)

Rumelt, Richard, *Good Strategy/Bad Strategy* (Profile Books, 2011)

Sherman, Michael, *The Mind of the Market* (Henry Holt and Company, 2008)

Smith, Richard, David King, Ranjit Sidhu & Dan Skelsey (editors), *The Effective Change Manager's Handbook* (Kogan Page, 2014)

Syed, Matthew, *Bounce: the Myth of Talent and the Power of Practice* (Fourth Estate, 2011)

Taleb, Nassim Nicholas, *The Black Swan* (Penguin, 2008)

The Economist, *Banco Santander, Pack Behaviour* (www.economist.com/node/12609706, accessed April 2016)

Toffler, Alvin, *Future Shock* (Pan Books, 1973)